STUCK

How to Overcome Your Anger and Reclaim Your Life

F. Remy Diederich

STUCK: How to Overcome Your Anger and Reclaim Your Life
by F. Remy Diederich

ALL RIGHTS RESERVED
No portion of this publication may be reproduced, stored in any electronic system or transmitted in any form or by any means, electronic, mechanical, photocopy, recording or otherwise, without the written permissions from the author and publisher. Brief quotations may be used in literary reviews

Unless otherwise indicated, all Scripture quotations are taken from the HOLY BIBLE, TODAY'S NEW INTERNATIONAL VERSION ® Copyright © 2001, 2005 by Biblica ®. Used by permission of Biblica ®. All rights reserved worldwide.

Scripture quotations marked (NIV) are taken from the Holy Bible, New International Version®, NIV®. Copyright © 1973, 1978, 1984, 2011 by Biblica, Inc ™ Used by permission of Zondervan. All rights reserved worldwide.

Scripture quotations marked (NLT) are taken from the Holy Bible, New Living Translation, copyright © 1996, 2004, 2007 by Tyndale House Foundation. Used by permission of Tyndale House Publishers, INC., Carol Stream, Illinois 60188. All Rights Reserved

Scripture quotations marked (KJV) are taken from the Holy Bible, King James Version. The KJV is public domain in the United States.

Copyright © 2012
by F. Remy Diederich
All Rights Reserved

ISBN-10: 1508838194
ISBN-13: 978-1508838197

Cover Design by: Jason Brooks
Cover Consultation Provided By: Andy Christensen
www.andrewjchristensen.com
Author photo courtesy of: Angie Green
www.angiegreenphotography.zenfolio.com

Be Sure To Check Out These Other Titles From F. Remy Diederich

Healing the Hurts of Your Past:
A Guide to Overcoming the Pain of Shame

www.readingremy.com/healing

Out of Exile
A Forty Day Journey from Setback to Comeback

www.readingremy.com/exile

*Dedicated to
Nicole, Daniel, and Zoe
Nate and Becca
May you always experience
and offer forgiveness freely.*

Table of Contents

How to Read This Book   1

Part One: STUCK   5

1. Spinning Your Wheels   8
2. Stuck in Anger   12
3. Seeing Anger   15
4. Understanding Anger   20
5. The Power to Choose   26
6. The Source of Anger   31
7. Anger Expressions   36
8. Seven Triggers That Tick You Off   39
9. Anger, Respect & Control   49
10. Stuck in Infectious Attitudes   54

11. Stuck in Denial   60
    - Breaking Through Denial   66

12. Stuck in Grief   69

13. Seven Factors That Keep You Stuck   75
    - Weak Boundaries   78
    - Shame   82
    - Narcissism   83
    - Passive-Aggressive Behavior   85
    - Indecision   87
    - Vows   88
    - Evil   90

Part Two: UNSTUCK 94

14. The Foolishness of Forgiveness 96
- Forgiveness: What It Is 98
- Forgiveness: What It Is Not 106

15. How to Forgive 114
- Be the Hero 115
- Two Beliefs to Help You Be the Hero 120

16. First Steps 126
- Don't Respond in Kind 127
- Step Back and Reflect 128
- Set Boundaries 131

17. Reframing 137
- Reframing the Offense 138
- Reframing the Results 146
- Eliminate Expectations 146
- Find the Silver Lining 149
- Reframing Your Identity 157

Part 3: Practical Steps 164

18. Having the Conversation 172
- Becoming a Peacemaker 173
- How to Confront Your Offender 183

19. When Nothing Works 190

20. Forgiveness and Beyond	**194**
• Blessing Your Offender	**198**

Part 4: The Other Side of Forgiveness — 203

21. How to Be Reconciled	**204**
• Forgiving Yourself	**216**
• Seven Reasons Why You Should Forgive Yourself	**217**
• How to Forgive Yourself	**220**
22. Closing Thoughts	**225**
23. Questions and Answers	**228**
Recommended Reading	**232**
Acknowledgements	**234**
About the Author	**237**

How to Read This Book

This isn't your typical self-help book. It's not about psychology, yet it contains many psychological truths. It's not about theology, yet it often quotes the Bible. It's not about theories or ideals. This book is a practical guide to help you overcome your anger and reclaim your life. STUCK is a manual to assist you in navigating the rough waters of conflict rather than remaining hopelessly stuck in them.

As pastor, counselor, and addiction consultant, I've worked with hundreds of people who have felt stuck and unable to move on with their lives. Their stories differ but typically have to do with another person: a parent, sibling, friend, co-worker, child, lover, or spouse. Something happened with a significant other to knock them off track, and life hasn't been the same ever since.

With these people in mind, I've pulled together the teaching and advice I have offered over the years to help them get unstuck. My hope is it can help you get unstuck as well.

I'm struck how this present generation lacks mentors, guides, and sages. These counselors exist, but we don't have the same access to them that we once did. Many of us grow up in broken families, often moving from place to place, overloaded with options from our media-rich world, and disconnected from the churches and civic organizations that once held us together and served as anchors for our lives. It's as if we have to find the answers to life on our own, reinventing the wheel with each problem we face. It can be a lonely place not knowing where to turn for some of the most basic and important decisions in life.

I hope this book will fill a gap in our culture by offering sound advice for people looking for answers to one of life's biggest questions: *What do I do with this broken relationship?*

I'll tell you right now, getting unstuck is hard work. There are no easy answers. You might not like my answers. You might be convinced I've got it all wrong; I just don't get it; what I suggest will never work. But if you trust me, I can help. *Really.* You might have to put the book down and come back in a day or two. Then again, it may be best to keep reading; what is unclear at first will probably make more sense when you read a broader context. In the end, I trust you will see the wisdom of what I have to say. Follow me, and I'll help you get your life back on track.

I can't take credit for any wisdom found in this book. I don't have an ounce of original thought. I'm merely a collator of wisdom from the Bible, research, other authors, my own personal experience, as well as stories from hundreds of people I've observed or counseled.

I'm a pastor at heart. I'm here to help you. My hope is this book will do more than help you resolve a broken relationship. I hope it will help you experience God in a new way as you invite him into your life to help you get unstuck.

Throughout the book I ask you to stop and "write it down" which means, answer the questions I offer to help internalize what you just read. Hint: the more questions you answer, the quicker you will get unstuck!

Also, feel free to jump to the spot in the book that resonates with you the most. I purposefully made the book scannable with short chapters, numbered points, and subheadings to help you fast-forward to special points of interest like: understanding your anger, learning how to forgive, overcoming grief, or how to forgive yourself. But I hope you will read through the initial chapters on anger because that information is foundational to the book.

I look forward to hearing from you with your comments and questions. My best days are when I get a note telling me how the words I shared helped change a life. Contact me at remydiederich@yahoo.com or through my blog at readingremy.com.

Part One

Stuck

Stuck in the mud.
Stuck in traffic.
Stuck in the middle.
Stuck in a blizzard.
Stuck at work.
Stuck in the past.
Stuck in a rut.
Stuck in a dead end job.
Stuck in marriage.
Stuck in life.

We've all been stuck. We all know the feeling.

Helpless.
Hopeless.
Overwhelmed.
Confused.
Ashamed.
Angry.
Exhausted.
Powerless.

You want to quit. You want someone to feel sorry for you and solve your problems so you don't have to. You want to wake up and have your problems all be gone.

Nice dream, but that's not reality, is it?

Even when you have the will to take action, you often don't know which action to take. Which is the right way to go? *When* should you go: now or later? What is *your* responsibility, and what is the responsibility of *others*? You've had so many misfires in the past. What's to make this time any different?

I live in Wisconsin. Everyone in Wisconsin gets stuck: in the snow, mostly. That's a part of life. It happens. We know what it takes to get unstuck. We're prepared. You get down on the ground with a shovel and tunnel out the snow from underneath your car. Then you throw down sand to get traction (it helps to travel with a bucket of sand in the trunk). If you can get someone to push you, that's great. Better yet, a group of people. If all else fails, have someone pull you out with a chain (yes, the chains go right next to the sand in the trunk).

My point is, there is an art and a process to getting unstuck. It's not always pretty, but when you are stuck you do what you have to do. Staring at the car doesn't help. Swearing at the car doesn't help. Calling your friends and complaining doesn't help either. If you want to get unstuck, then get to work. You can rest but not for long. The longer you wait, the longer it takes to get back on the road. Deal with it. Give it your best shot. You may even need to call a tow truck. But do whatever it takes, and eventually you'll be on your way.

Do nothing, and you go nowhere.

Are you stuck?
If you are holding this book you must be stuck. Something happened, and you just can't seem to find enough traction to get on with your life. It might be a serious violation like rape, the death of a loved one, or a relational betrayal: an affair or divorce. Or it might be less dramatic but still hurtful: the loss of a job, the death of a pet, a cross-country move, etc.

You've tried complaining and blaming. You've tried feeling sorry for yourself and possibly medicating your pain with drugs and/or alcohol. It may have gotten so bad you considered, or actually attempted, taking your life. But having tried these things you realize now they only took you deeper, making you more stuck.

You've wasted so much time. But don't give up. There's hope. You have many good years left…if you do something about it now. *Today.*

Let's Get Started

I am privileged you have invited me into your life at this important time. It could be your defining moment. Now let's see if we can get you unstuck.

Chapter One:

Spinning Your Wheels

In the movie, *Forrest Gump*, we get a great picture of people that are stuck. In my first book,[1] I looked at how Lieutenant Dan was stuck in shame. Now I want to look at another character: Jenny. She was stuck in *anger.*

When Forrest is just a boy, Jenny is his best friend. One day Jenny invites Forrest over to her house. Jenny meets him in her front yard, grabs Forrest's hand, and goes racing through the back yard into the cornfield behind her house. As the two children fight their way through the corn stalks Jenny's dad comes out the back door with a whiskey bottle in one hand and yells out, "Jenny! Jenny, you come back

---

[1] F. Remy Diederich, *Healing the Hurts of Your Past* (Cross Point Publishing)

here!"

Jenny doesn't listen. The two keep running until they collapse out of exhaustion. Then Jenny repeats a prayer, "God, make me a bird so I can fly far, far away." Throughout the movie Forrest narrates what's going on; he explains here saying, "God didn't make Jenny a bird, but the po-lice did come and took her daddy away."

Jenny goes to live with her grandmother. It was never explicitly stated, but you got the point. Jenny's dad abused her sexually.

Fast forward to Jenny's late teens and early twenties. Jenny's pain is evident. Her life is characterized by alcohol and drug addiction, a series of abusive boyfriends, suicide attempts, and stripping in a club. Looking for some peace and sanity, she goes to visit Forrest who had taken over his mother's southern mansion after her death.

Jenny spends the weekend recuperating: mostly sleeping. Then Forrest and Jenny take a long walk. They enjoy spending time with each other and the beautiful day until Jenny looks up and realizes she's at the driveway of her childhood home. She freezes for a moment then starts to walk down the long gravel driveway. Forrest lets her go, knowing that she's got some business to do with her deceased father.

As Jenny walks toward the house you can see her pretty face turn ugly. It begins to contort in bitterness as her childhood memories start to play out in her mind. When she gets within throwing distance of the house, Jenny takes one of the sandals she's been carrying and throws it as hard as she can at the house. But it's so light it barely makes a sound. She throws the other sandal with the same effect. In desperation she looks at the ground for something more substantial to throw. She finds a rock and throws it, then another, and another.

Finally, one of the rocks hits a window, breaking it but giving her no satisfaction. Frustrated, she falls to the ground and weeps. Meanwhile, Forrest has been slowly walking down the driveway. He kneels down behind her and gently touches her shoulders, not knowing what to do or say. Narrating again he says, "S*ome days there just aren't enough rocks."*

What did Forrest mean by that: *Some days there just aren't enough rocks?*

Sometimes throwing rocks *can* help. It can relieve the stress of life's frustrations. For example, I like to run and work out for that reason. In fact, a doctor once told me an hour-long workout is the equivalent of taking one anti-depressant. But there are other times throwing rocks won't help. The pain is too deep. The wound is too raw.

Jenny was stuck.

Her wheels were spinning, but she had no traction. She expended a lot of energy but to no effect.

What her father started she now perpetuated. Her father wasn't keeping her chained to her past: *she was*...by her thoughts and the decisions she made every day. She needed something much more sophisticated than a rock throwing session. She needed a process to help her break free from the past and move on to claim her future.

A Process
My guess is you need the same process. We all do.

That's the goal of this book, to give you a reliable process to help you move on from the hurts of your past. This process includes the discussion of anger but also loss, grief, forgiveness, and faith. We will explore some difficult topics, topics that might open the door to freedom and even joy if you are willing to walk through them.

I hope you will resolve right now to not stay stuck. Nothing good will come from that.

A Faith-Based Approach
This book is rooted in biblical thought and faith in God, but you can relax. You don't have to believe in God or be a devout believer to get something out of this book. The principles I offer will help you no matter what you believe about God. My goal isn't to preach at you or

convert you. I've been teaching this material in a secular environment for years (minus the biblical references) with great effect. But if you want the most power to help you get unstuck then please consider inviting God to help you. If what you've tried so far hasn't helped, it may be worth trying a new approach that includes God.

Write it down:

- *Have you ever felt that "some days there just aren't enough rocks"? What led you to experience that kind of anger?*

- *Who or what would you like to throw rocks at if you could?*

- *Do feel like you are stuck in your past? What is keeping you stuck?*

- *Are you ready to get unstuck?*

- Take a minute to consider what it is you are looking to get out of this book. *What is the goal you want to achieve?*

- *What do you want your life to look like? In other words, what would life look like to you if you could get unstuck? How might it look in five, ten, or twenty years from now?*

- *What will your life look like in five, ten, or twenty years if you stay stuck?*

Chapter Two

Stuck in Anger

It's easy to get stuck. First you experience a loss, and then your emotions grab you and chain you to that loss...*sometimes for years*.

Fear, sadness, and anger are the main emotions that get you stuck. My primary focus in this book is on anger.

> Lewis Smedes, author of *Forgive and Forget*, paints a vivid picture of what it's like to get stuck in anger. He compares it to trapping yourself in a torture chamber:
>
>> Recall the pain of being wronged, the hurt of being stung, cheated, demeaned. Doesn't the memory of it fuel the fire of fury again, make it hurt again? Suppose you never forgive, suppose you feel the hurt each time your memory lights on the people who did you wrong. And suppose you have a

> compulsion to think of them constantly. You have become a prisoner of your past pain; you are locked into a torture chamber of your own making. Time should have left your pain behind; but you keep it alive to let it flay you over and over.
>
> Your own memory is a replay of your hurt; a videotape within your soul that plays unending reruns of your old rendezvous with pain. You cannot switch it off. You are hooked into it like a pain junkie; you become addicted to your remembrance of past pain. You are lashed again each time your memory spins the tape. Is this fair to yourself; this wretched justice of not forgiving? You could not be more unfair to yourself. [2]

Can you relate to that? Have you put yourself in the torture chamber of unforgiveness? Anger and unforgiveness, by their very nature, lock on to the past. These words, along with other words like resentment, bitterness, hatred, and envy are "stuck" words: words that keep you trapped in your past. Whenever you hear yourself using or thinking these words, you are in dangerous territory. Start looking for a way out.

Tim Allen knows what it means to be stuck in anger. Tim was the star of the hit TV show *Home Improvement*. He told his story in *Parade* magazine a few years ago. He said when his dad was killed in a car accident, his world was turned upside down, and he immediately became angry. He describes the impact it had on him:
> It hit me hard. I didn't see it coming, didn't understand it, and it hurt like hell. Why would God take my father away? Then came the guilt and anger. I kept looking around for someone to help me deal with these feelings. I needed taking care of, but nobody was going to do it. Nobody in my family spoke much about it. There was nobody in school or the neighborhood like me. From then on, I cut myself adrift. It was like I was going down the same river as everyone else, only now I was no longer in the same vessel. I was alone. [3i]

---

[2] Lewis Smedes, *Forgive and Forget: Healing the Hurts We Don't Deserve,* (Ballantine Books), pages 132,133
[3] *Facing My Fear of Intimacy.* (*Parade* magazine), October 27, 2002.

What a picture of isolation and despair. Allen tells how growing up he fell in with a bad crowd and started using and selling drugs. He was arrested and sent to prison for over two years. When he got out, comedy became his salvation. He said the only place he felt comfortable was in front of an audience. He became incredibly famous and wealthy from *Home Improvement,* but his drinking got out of control, ending his twelve-year marriage, and putting him in a treatment center.

Thankfully, Tim was able to get sober. He said he found healing in the presence of his daughter:

> I adore being in the house with my daughter...being silent, doing my art; just knowing she's near. It's the best connection – it's unconditional. My daughter eases the ache I used alcohol to calm. Because of her, this void at the center of things since my father died started to fill up. My daughter slowly crept up on me, removing the obstacles to connection.[4]

Tim's story shows how you don't have to stay stuck in anger. You can move beyond the pain of your past. When I first read this story I was concerned that Tim might be tempted to merely *salve* his pain with the help of his daughter without *solving* it. It's tempting to move just far enough down the road where you relieve your pain without truly getting free. I was pleased to read a recent article about Tim where he expressed that he has continued to find healing, and his spirituality has played a significant role in the process.[5]

Write it down:

- How have you made yourself a prisoner of past pain?

- What is it about Tim Allen's story that you can relate to?

- Are you content to salve your pain, or are you willing to solve it?

---

[4] Ibid.
[5] *The Truth About Tim Allen*, AARP the magazine, October/November 2012

Chapter Three:

Seeing Anger

Anger scares us. Because it scares us, we avoid it. We avert our eyes, hoping that if we ignore it, anger won't bother us.

But avoiding anger doesn't change the reality of its existence. It's there. We need to open our eyes and deal with it.

Let me ask you a few questions to help you to start seeing anger.

1. The Look Of Anger
When you think of anger, what comes to mind? In other words, what does anger look like to you?
- Rage?
- Violence?
- Swearing?

- Silence?
- Sadness?

Anger affects everyone in a different way. Because of that, we don't always recognize it. For me, anger disguised itself as frustration. I read once where a psychologist said he never used the word "frustrated". Not only would he not use the word, he didn't allow anyone in his practice to use the word either. Why? Because he thought the word "frustrated" was a substitute for "anger". As long as people can describe themselves as "frustrated" they will never admit to being angry. It is a form of denial. When I read that it hit me between the eyes because I always used the word "frustrated" to describe how I felt.

I was in a leadership meeting at church once. We were sitting around a small coffee table, and I had a Styrofoam cup of coffee sitting on it. Something came up in the meeting that was a recurring problem in the church. I said, "I am so frustrated!" At the same time I hit the coffee table with my fist, and the cup went flying.

I wasn't *frustrated*. I was *angry*, but I didn't want to admit it because *angry* wasn't something I thought I should be. Anger was something ugly, something "unchristian". When my dad got angry he would swear and say demeaning things to people. I didn't want to be like that. I took my anger undercover and called it "frustration".

Write it down:

- *What does anger look like in your life?*

- *How have you taken your anger undercover?*

- *How have you relabeled your anger to make it more acceptable?*

2. The Feel Of Anger

Here's another question, how do you *feel* about anger? Does it scare you? Embarrass you? Make you sad?

Most people are ashamed of their anger. They associate anger with losing control, conflict, or broken relationships. Anger makes them feel guilty. In fact, many people will never pick up a book on anger because they don't want anyone to think they have a problem with it. They may not even want to admit it to themselves. They spend their lives running from anger and conflict, leaving a wake of relationships that are broken, superficial, and unfulfilling.

Write it down:

- *How do you feel about anger?*

- *Have you run from anger rather than resolve it?*

3. The Impact Of Anger

One last question, how do you think anger impacts our culture? Here are a few areas you'll find anger every day:

The news. Pick up any newspaper on any day, and you will easily find a dozen articles rooted in anger. When you read about road rage, divorce, and wars, you are reading about anger. For example, as I write today, the trending story is about T.J. Lane. T.J. is a 17-year-old boy charged with three juvenile counts of aggravated murder for shooting five students in an Ohio high school.

Sports. You see anger in baseball when the benches clear for a fight. You see it in hockey when the players drop their gloves. A few years back, I was shocked to hear how professional basketball players went into the stands to fight the fans. And in Minnesota last year a hockey dad was convicted of attacking and choking his son's coach.[6]

---

[6] http://minnesota.cbslocal.com/2011/12/22/hockey-dad-charged-with-choking-sons-coach/

Television. What shows do you think about when you think of anger? *Judge Judy. Jerry Springer. Divorce Court. COPS*. In my seminars I always ask my audience which shows reflect anger. On one occasion a man responded with "*Seinfeld*". That really surprised me. No one had ever mentioned *Seinfeld* before. I asked him why he thought of *Seinfeld,* and he challenged me to think of any episode. Almost all of the humor on *Seinfeld* is based on anger. I didn't believe him at first, but as I thought through different episodes, he was right. Elaine, George, Jerry, and Kramer were always mad at someone, and their anger was the basis for the show's humor: the springboard for their punch lines. As I thought about other sitcoms, I realized that anger is the basis for a great deal of TV humor.

Music. Can you think of any music that is associated with anger? Maybe Rap or Heavy Metal? They might be the first genres to come to mind, but keep thinking. Have you ever heard an angry country song? Oh yeah. Read the chorus of Carrie Underwood's song, *Before He Cheats*:

> I dug my key into the side
> Of his pretty little souped-up 4 wheel drive
> Carved my name into his leather seats
> I took a Louisville slugger to both headlights
> Slashed a hole in all 4 tires
> And maybe next time he'll think before he cheats

Every music genre has anger, even classical. Why? Because music expresses our soul, and our soul is often filled with anger.

The legal system. Where would the legal system be without anger? Just think how many court cases are the result of people trying to get back at someone with a lawsuit.

The list of anger in the culture goes on and on. What about anger in art, religion, politics, and traffic? Once you start to see anger, you will find it everywhere you turn because we are angry people looking for ways to express our anger.

Anger Keeps Us Stuck

We live in an anger-saturated culture. Because it is saturated, we don't always see anger even when it is in front of us; no more than a fish sees water right in front of it. Since anger is ever-present, we look right past it. And since there is always someone angrier than we are, it is easy to justify the anger we have. As a result, it's easy to get stuck in anger and not even realize it. We've normalized anger to the point that we don't see it is the glue that keeps us stuck in our past.

Write it down:

- It's important that you are able to see anger in our culture in order to be aware of how anger is constantly influencing you. List other examples of anger that you see around you every day.

- *Do you minimize your anger because you see it so much elsewhere?*

Chapter Four:

Understanding Anger

Anger is a tricky emotion. Its power can confuse and intimidate you, causing you to shut down and become stuck.

Understanding your anger is the first step to getting unstuck.

There are many misunderstandings about anger. Forget what you know or think you know about anger for a few minutes. This chapter is meant to help you get a fresh perspective. I'll start with my definition of anger:

> Anger is a God-given emotional response to injustice. It is an emotion that motivates and empowers you to defend what is good and true. Anger compels you to right wrongs.

Dr. David Seamands, author of *Healing for Damaged Emotions*, defines

anger this way:
> Anger is a divinely implanted emotion. Closely allied to our instinct for right, it is designed to be used for constructive spiritual purposes. The person who cannot feel anger at evil is a person who lacks enthusiasm for good. If you cannot hate wrong, it's very questionable whether you really love righteousness.[7]

My guess is you never heard anger defined in such positive terms. Most of us think of anger as something bad: something destructive. And I bet you never heard that anger is from God! Maybe you heard about Jesus being angry, but it always made you a little uncomfortable, like it shouldn't be in the Bible, right? Let's take a look at that now.

When Jesus Got Angry

There are three examples of Jesus getting angry, all in the book of Mark. The first example is when the religious rulers of the day didn't want Jesus to heal anyone on the Sabbath. Mark tells us:
> ...some of them were looking for a reason to accuse Jesus so they watched him closely... Mark 3:2

Then Mark says Jesus:
> ...looked around at them in anger... because he was deeply distressed at their stubborn hearts... Mark 3:5

Another occasion is when people brought their children to Jesus, but his disciples told them to go away. Mark said:
> When Jesus saw this, he was indignant. He said to them "Let the little children come to me, and do not hinder them, for the kingdom of God belongs to such as these." Mark 10:14

The third occurrence is when Jesus entered the temple to find people setting up a market. Jesus overturned tables and drove people away incensed at what they had done to God's house of worship [Mark 11:15].

Either it's wrong that Jesus got angry or there are times when anger is

---

[7] Dr. David Seamands, *Healing for Damaged Emotions*, (David C. Cook)

appropriate behavior. I believe the latter. In each story Jesus became angry in the face of some kind of *injustice*. In each story his anger moved him to *confront* injustice. Note that he didn't hold onto the anger and become bitter. Jesus didn't use his anger as an excuse to lose control, become abusive, or destructive. The anger came, it moved him to address specific injustices, and then he let it go. In other words:

>   *Jesus experienced anger.*
>   *Jesus expressed anger.*
>   *Jesus let his anger go.*

Anger doesn't have to be a bad emotion with bad results. It's a God given emotion to resolve injustice. This should be our model for how we deal with anger.

Write it down:

- *Have you ever thought of anger in a positive way?*

- *Have you ever thought of anger as God-given?*

- *How does this definition of anger change your thinking about anger?*

- *What's different about the way Jesus expressed his anger and the way you express yours?*

The Anger Process

Jesus' approach to handling anger is a lot different from our approach. In fact, I want to break the anger process down so you can see exactly where it is we go wrong.

Anger progresses in three stages:

Stage One: Anger starts when you perceive an injustice. *Perceive* is the key word here because your perception may be wrong, but you still get angry.

Stage Two: Once you perceive an injustice you immediately have the emotional response of anger. Anger, at some level, will always result when an injustice is perceived. You can't help it. This is a part of who God made you to be. You do not have to feel guilty about experiencing this emotion. In fact, you should be more concerned if you don't have an anger response to injustice.

Stage Three: The purpose of anger is to move you to take action. If anger doesn't evoke a response from you that means you internalized your anger or what is often called: *stuffing your anger*.

Perceived Injustice > Emotional Response > Action Taken

This is the anger process. Where we go wrong, and where anger gets all the bad press, is in the space between the emotional response and the action taken. We go wrong for primarily two reasons.

First, we fail to ask if our perception is accurate. We rush to judgment and take action without thinking things through. For example, let's say you have a child who comes home from school and tells you his teacher ridiculed him openly in front of his class. That's a serious accusation. If it's true, it's definitely an injustice, and you have every right to be angry.

But what if it's not true? What if your child misread the situation? Before you accept the anger you want to first clarify what happened. Did your child misread what actually happened? A simple phone call might be all it takes to determine if your child's accusation is true or false.

Perceived Injustice > Emotional Response > Action Taken
- **True**
- **False**

We often make a mistake by taking a small amount of information and jumping to conclusions. To justify our conclusion, we fabricate why we think our anger is appropriate, creating excuses that may not be true. In fact, studies have shown that when you are angry, your mind seeks to justify your anger.[8] That is, rather than your mind slowing you down, cautioning you to make sure you perceived an injustice accurately, the opposite happens. Your mind is convinced that an injustice has absolutely occurred and *looks* for evidence to prove it. Knowing this, be very careful in letting yourself get angry in the first place because once you become angry it's hard to back down.

My point here is that when you experience anger, your first step should be to question whether or not you have any right to be angry. The Bible gives an excellent example of this. The prophet Jonah got mad at God for wanting to rescue a group of people called the Ninevites. God questioned Jonah's anger saying:

>Is it right for you to be angry? Jonah 4:4

That's the question we should always ask ourselves the minute we experience the heat of anger rise up in our chest...*is it right to be angry? Did I perceive things accurately? Was there really an injustice? Do I have all the facts? Did I jump to a conclusion or rush to judgment?*

The moment you feel anger is an excellent time to invite God to help you gain clarity before your emotion sends you in the wrong direction. Pray something like this:

>*Father, I'm mad about this. Help me to get to the bottom of this problem and find out if it's true or not. I don't want to get angry or take action until I know all the facts.*

Failing to judge your perception is the first mistake we make.

---

[8] Paul Ekman, *Emotions Revealed,* (Holt Paperbacks), p. 39

The second mistake we make is defaulting to retaliation. Most people have not been trained in how to respond to anger nor has it been modeled for them growing up. They live by the motto "If it feels good, do it." If it feels good to yell, then yell. If it feels good to slander, then slander. If it feels good to throw something, then throw something. Any action seems justified by the offense, but retaliation never solves anything.

Write it down:

- *As you assess your anger, do you think it's more often based on true perception or false?* Explain.

- *Are you too quick to perceive an injustice? Why do you think that is?*

- *Do you rush to judgment and jump to conclusions?*

- *Do people often tell you that you misunderstood them?*

- *Do you automatically default to retaliation?*

- *As you look at past retaliation, how has it made things worse for you?*

Chapter Five:

The Power to Choose

When you experience anger, you have a choice. You may only have a split second to choose, but that's why it is so important to know the opportunity exists.

Too many people say things like, "I couldn't help myself. I *had* to get angry and say what I did," etc. That's not true. You have a moment to choose; so seize the moment and choose well.

To make our equation accurate there needs to be another word inserted into the process. It's the word "choice." There are a couple of choices that need to be made.

Perceived Injustice > Emotional Response > CHOICE > Action Taken

There are a couple of choices that need to be made.

Appropriate Or Inappropriate?

In the heat of the moment, you must decide if your anger is appropriate or inappropriate. If you have misperceived the situation, you will be angry without cause. If you are smart, you will swallow your pride, power down, and admit that you made a mistake. But many times you are so invested in your error that you are unwilling to back down. You push through with your accusations and condemnations, only to make a bad situation worse.

If your anger is appropriate, then congratulations; you have the right to be angry! The emotion is justified, but not any *action* is justified. Many people think that just because they have a right to be angry it entitles them to any behavior or attitude they choose. Not at all. They still need to act appropriately so their behavior is helpful and not hurtful, and from a spiritual side, they would hopefully want to act in a way that honors God.

Constructive Or Destructive?

Another choice to make in this moment is whether you will be *constructive* or *destructive*. Anyone can be destructive. No skill or character is required. But it takes grace, wisdom, and self-control to know how to confront an injustice constructively. You want to *solve* the problem, not enflame it. Think of putting out a fire. You can run to a fire with a bucket of water or a bucket of gasoline. Too many people grab the wrong bucket and the fire explodes instead of being extinguished.

If God granted me three wishes, one of them would be to have the power to help people in the seconds between their "emotional response" and the "action taken" in the anger process. I would love to pull people aside and counsel them in that moment, helping them to accurately assess what just happened and make wise choices. Much relational damage would be averted, as well as physical damage, career damage, etc.

Help From Above

I can't be there to help you, but God can. He sends his Spirit to guide and empower you in these moments. His Spirit is present to manifest himself in your life. That is what the Bible means when it says:
> ...the fruit of the Spirit is love, joy, peace, patience, kindness, goodness, faithfulness, gentleness and self-control. Galatians 5:22,23

The Spirit comes to help you in your weakness. Notice how the fruit of the Spirit is related to peace-making behavior: *love, joy, peace, patience, kindness, goodness, faithfulness, gentleness, and self-control.* God shows up in your life in a way that promotes peace and unity with other people.

Responding To Injustice

I want to return to my schoolteacher analogy from before. You were able to hold off your anger until you got more information. That's good. You went to the teacher and talked to her. Or maybe you spoke to other children in the class to get an eyewitness account and learned that your child was right; the teacher did ridicule your son in front of the class.

You have a right to be angry because that indeed is an injustice. *But what will you do about it? How will you respond?* This is where many of us fail. We let the emotion of anger empower us, but we use the power to be *de*-structive not *con*-structive. We use it to work vengeance and retaliate instead of working to solve the problem, which only creates more difficulties for us.

It's important to see that in the moment of anger you have an opportunity to choose. Again, it may only be a second, but it's enough to do the right thing. *Will you act appropriately or inappropriately?*

Will you be constructive or destructive? Will you honor God in the moment or dishonor him?

Perceived Injustice > Emotional Response > CHOICE > Action Taken
- Constructive
- Destructive

It's in these moments of choice that you can ask God for help. Pray something like this:

> *Father, please help me see clearly. What do I need to know about this situation? How do You want me to respond? What will bring honor to You in this situation? Help me bring Your kingdom of peace and justice and not my kingdom of destruction. Help me to bring a solution and not just add to the problem.*

Your goal is not to work justice. That's ultimately God's responsibility. Your job is to *confront* injustice: point it out, and then turn it over to those in control. In the case of the teacher, you might be able to resolve the issue on your own. She may offer you an explanation and/or an apology that satisfies you. If she doesn't, then take it to the principal or school board: charge *them* with pursuing justice. You have done your part in confronting injustice; now let it go.

The problem is, sometimes you can't let it go. You hold onto your anger, and it turns to bitterness, resentment, and even hatred. You spend days, months, and sometimes years reworking the events in your mind. Retaliation naturally follows, whether actual or imagined. To make matters worse, friends and family are often present to cheer you on in your behavior.

This pattern always leaves you stuck.

But it doesn't have to. You have a choice.

The Bible understands your natural tendency to let your anger get the best of you. That's why says:

> In your anger do not sin: Do not let the sun go down while you

are still angry, and do not give the devil a foothold. Ephesians 4:26,27

To be angry and not sin, *is that even possible?* It is. God wants you to be angry at injustice, but he doesn't want you to sin as you respond to it. He doesn't want you to retaliate and hurt others. That only adds to the problem. He wants you to *resolve* the problem.

Write it down:

- *How do you respond to injustice? Do you seek resolution or retaliation?*

- *Do your efforts bring closure, or do they just make matters worse?*

- *Do you invite God's presence to help you, or do you work things out based on what feels good in the moment?*

- *Who are the people in your life that encourage you to retaliate?*

- Come up with an action plan to choose well when you experience the first sign of anger. *What steps can you take that will cause you to stop, pray, think, and choose well?*

Chapter Six:

The Source of Anger

I've mapped out the anger process. Now I want to look at the source of anger to help you gain more clarity.

Every day you have hundreds of expectations on how your day will go: who will call, how people will treat you, if your team will win, if your loved one will live, if your picnic will get rained out, if you will get a raise, etc. But your reality doesn't always meet your expectations. It often falls short. It looks like this:

<u>Expectations</u>

<u>　Reality　</u>

If you are emotionally and spiritually mature, this shortfall is not an issue. You know how to adapt. You know how to raise your performance to reach your expectations, lower your expectations to be more realistic, or even suspend your expectations knowing that expectations can be counterproductive.

This is asking a lot from the average person. Most of us experience a tension when our reality doesn't measure up to what we expect. The difference between our expectation and our reality is considered an injustice; at least it's an injustice to us. When our expectations aren't met we say, *That's not fair! That's not the way my life is supposed to be.*

Another more basic term for injustice is simply "loss." Whenever you experience loss you experience the accompanying emotions, one of which is anger. The greater the loss: the greater the anger. Your first reaction might be to deny this; you don't believe that loss always causes anger. But that's only because you aren't *aware* of the emotion. People tend to think of anger as a big emotion, but it can be understated too.

The next time you experience a loss take inventory of how you feel. At a minimum there is a sigh, a grimace, or a rolling of the eyes revealing the anger present.

You don't have to feel bad or guilty about this reaction. It's just the way you were created. The emotion of anger helps you to right a wrong. It's simply the irritation that comes from something not being right. It happens with small and big losses. It's what drives you to take action against the injustice.

The Anger Behind The Anger

Let's drill down a little deeper to find the true source of anger. What I want you to see here is that the initial loss you experience isn't always what hurts the most. There is often anger behind the anger. I'll explain it with a story.

When my children were very young, we lived on a farm. I remember coming home one night from the barn and finding their toys scattered in the yard. I didn't like how it looked. I went in the house and told my kids to get out there and put things away. They scrambled outside and picked things up. Point made.

The next night I came home and it was déjà vu. The toys were out, and the kids were inside for the night. I went in the house and immediately scolded them for leaving the yard a mess. I wasn't happy that I had to tell them two nights in a row, and my tone made it clear.

Now, this is what I want you to see. The loss I experienced was a messy yard, but my reaction bothered me. It felt like the crime didn't justify my level of anger. I wondered if there might not be something deeper going on inside of me. I turned my wonder into a prayer; *God, what's going on? What do I need to see here? What am I missing?*

Primary And Secondary Losses

After reflecting on my anger, I discovered there was indeed something deeper. I found anger behind my anger. The messy yard was just the tip of the iceberg, or what I call the *primary loss*. There were other losses just beneath the surface, or what I call *secondary losses*:

First, there was a *loss of respect*. I didn't feel that my kids were listening to me. If they respected me they wouldn't leave the yard a mess. (Or so I thought at the time.)

Second, there was a *loss of control*. We lived in a mobile home, and we were very poor. I was ashamed of how poor we were and that I couldn't solve our financial problems. To be honest, when I saw the messy yard, our home looked like what people call "trailer trash." I was embarrassed, and I felt personally responsible for our poverty.

Yet a third loss was the *quality of my parenting*. I was so busy working on the farm I feared my kids weren't listening to me because I wasn't around enough to earn their respect. I thought I was a bad dad and feared my kids knew it.

When I saw these three losses I realized the messy yard was only a small part of my anger. I was mad at myself because I believed the lies that the messy yard was telling me: *I'm a bad dad, a bad provider,* and *I've lost the respect of my children.* It looks like this.

When I saw this, I guessed about eighty percent of my anger came from the secondary losses while only twenty percent came from the primary loss (the messy yard). Yet my children took the brunt of my anger. That was a defining moment for me as both parent and human being. I determined not to let my secondary losses hijack my emotions and behavior anymore.

What about you? What is the anger behind your anger?

Write it down:
Many people aren't aware of their losses. As a result, they don't understand where their anger comes from. A simple exercise helps. Sit down and write out the losses in your life. Start with the primary loss and then add the secondary losses. You will be surprised how quickly the losses add up.

For example, consider the losses that might result from your parents divorcing. The primary loss is the break-up of your parental unit, but there are many secondary losses. Here are just a few:
- Loss of income, which might mean the loss of cherished activities (sports, band, vacations) or loss of your home.
- Loss of a home might mean a move, which in turn causes the loss of friends, school, church, and other involvements.
- Plus, there are the intangible losses such as a sense of belonging, a sense of security, trust, etc.

If you take time to write out all the losses you have incurred throughout your life it will quickly become apparent why you have issues of anger. Look at your life in five-year segments starting from birth and work your way to the present writing out your losses.

Years: Birth – Five
- Primary loss: (example: parents' divorce, parents were alcoholics, abuse)
- Secondary losses:

Years: Six – Ten
- Primary loss: (example: parents' divorce, moved to a new town, illness)
- Secondary losses:

Years: Eleven – Fifteen
- Primary loss: (example: dropped out of sports, lost a close friend)
- Secondary losses:

Years: Sixteen – Twenty
- Primary loss: (example: got pregnant, dropped out of college, injury)
- Secondary losses:

Years: Twenty – one – Thirty
- Primary loss: (example: death of a friend, divorce, unable to have children)
- Secondary losses:

Chapter Seven:

Anger Expressions

We've looked at where anger comes from. Now let's see what it looks like when it manifests. People express their anger in primarily three ways:

> They blow up.
> They clam up.
> They have a slow release.

Of course there are many expressions of anger, but these are the main categories. I like to compare the anger experience to a can of pop. Shake a pop can, and open it up. What happens? It blows up. It gets all over and leaves a mess. Is that what your anger looks like? Or are you more like the shaken can that isn't opened: full of pressure with no outlet?

Author Jay Adams describes it this way:

> Righteous anger can become unrighteous anger in two ways: 1) by ventilation of anger 2) by the internalization of anger.

These two opposite extremes are known more popularly as blowing up and clamming up… In both cases, the emotional energies of anger are wasted. In both they are used "destructively." In neither instance are they used constructively to solve problems.[9]

Blowing up is nothing to take lightly. It can get you in a lot of trouble. Maybe you know firsthand what that's about!

There's a story in the Bible about David and a rich man named Nabal. David and his men acted like a small army protecting Nabal and his herds of cattle. When David needed food and provisions, he sent his men to Nabal to ask for a returned favor. But Nabal had no time for David, rejecting his request.

David was livid. He blew up and prepared to kill Nabal. Thankfully Nabal's wife, Abigail, intervened and calmed David down. She saved not only Nabal from death but also David from ruining his reputation as God's chosen leader. The entire chapter (1 Samuel 25) is worth a look to study anger and peacemaking skills.

There's a better way to express your anger than blowing up like David. Think of an aerosol spray container instead of a shaken pop can. Even though both cans are under pressure, the aerosol can doesn't make a mess when you press the button. Why? Because the button provides a mechanism that gives you a controlled release. That's what you want for your anger: a mechanism that gives you a controlled release. Such a mechanism allows your anger to be constructive and not destructive.

Aristotle said:
> Anybody can become angry – that is easy; but to be angry with the right person, and to the right degree, and at the right time, and for the right purpose, and in the right way – that is not within everybody's power and is not easy.

---

[9] Jay Adams, *The Christian Counselors Manual*, (Zondervan), chapter 31

I will talk more about how to offer a controlled release in the pages ahead.

Write it down:

- *How do you release your anger? Do you blow up, clam up, or have a slow release?*

- *Why do you think that is?*

- *What types of situations cause you to blow up? Clam up? Experience a slow release?*

- *What outcomes typically follow these three responses to anger?*

Chapter Eight:

Seven Triggers That Tick You Off

Earlier I introduced you to the anger behind the anger: what I called primary and secondary losses. I want to explore this idea more to help you better understand what's at the heart of your anger.

When I initially did my anger research I was overwhelmed with the many sources of anger. I listed out countless reasons why people get angry and then labeled each one. I grouped types that were similar and slowly pared my listing down to seven categories of anger triggers. My hope was that, if I could sort the causes for anger, I might find some universal truth about anger. I actually did. When you get to the end of this chapter, maybe you will have the same "ah-ha moment" I did.

Following are seven categories, or "triggers", that tick you off. They are not all-inclusive but should help you to better understand your anger.

1. Invalidation

Invalidation means to negate the value of something. It means to overlook, put down, take for granted, or reject something because you believe it has little or no value.

We are all created with the stamp of God's image on our lives. Therefore, we have inherent value. Many of us recognize our value, if only at a subconscious level, setting up an expectation that we will be shown respect. When someone contradicts our expectation by invalidating us, we experience a loss. That's where the hurt and anger come from. Something inside rises up and objects: *This is wrong! How can you say that to me? How can you treat me like that? Can't you see that I have value?*

Earlier I referenced a Bible story where Nabal humiliated David. Nabal made David feel small and insignificant when he said:
> Who is this David? Who is this son of Jesse? Many servants are breaking away from their masters these days. Why should I take my bread and water, and the meat I have slaughtered for my shearers, and give it to men coming from who knows where? 1 Samuel 25:10,11

Nabal said David was nothing special: just one of many. This invalidation infuriated David. All the protection that David offered Nabal's men and sheep was discounted with just a few words prompting David's intense anger. Isn't it amazing how words can set us off so easily?

Invalidation is often at the root of anger. In fact, marriage researchers at the University of Denver found invalidation is one of four key causes to marriage breakdowns.[10] Invalidation doesn't come from verbal put-downs alone but actions like offering unsolicited advice or questioning motives, which make a person feel disrespected by their mate.

---

[10] Stanley, Trathen, McCain, *A Lasting Promise*, (Bryan, Jossey-Bass), p. 32-35

What is it about being invalidated that ticks us off? Think of the secondary losses. Respect and a sense of dignity are at the top of the list.

Notice that I make a distinction between "dignity" and "a sense of dignity." Respect is something I give you. Dignity is something God gives you. Dignity is what makes you worthy of respect. It's your inherent value. I can't take your dignity, and you can't lose it, but I can make you doubt it. So the loss is a "sense" of dignity, not the dignity itself.

Invalidation can also cause you to feel a loss of control. You want so much to stop the person who is hurting you, but you can't. You have no control over them. It's like watching Simon Cowell in the early days of the television show *American Idol*. He could be so cruel with his cutting remarks. When Simon belittled contestants I'm sure they wanted to turn off his microphone, but they couldn't. They had to sit there and take it. His words could end their careers, and they knew it. It must have been humiliating, and it angered many of them.

What you expected: respect and esteem.
What you got: invalidation and rejection.
What you lost: respect, control, and a sense of dignity.

2. Personal Trauma

In his book, *A Grace Disguised*, Jerry Sittser tells the story of how three members of his family were taken in one tragic car accident. This is what he said about loss after experiencing his own:

> We live life as if it were a motion picture. Loss turns life into a snapshot. The movement stops; everything freezes. We find ourselves looking at picture albums to remember the motion picture of our lives that once was but can no longer be. [11]

Loss turns life into a snapshot. That's an interesting metaphor. Lenore Terr, author of *Too Scared to Cry*, uses another film analogy:

> The memory of trauma is shot with higher intensity light than is ordinary memory. And the film doesn't seem to disintegrate

---

[11] Jerry Sittser, *A Grace Disguised*, Expanded Version, (Zondervan), p. 93

with the usual half-life of ordinary film. Only the best lenses are used, lenses that will pick up every last detail, every line, every wrinkle, and every fleck. There is more detail picked up during traumatic events than one would expect from the naked eye under ordinary circumstances.[12]

That's what happened with Sittser. His life was moving along fine, like a motion picture, until the car crash. Then he was handed a snapshot of loss to always remind him of what once was but can no longer be. He comments on how anger relates to loss:

> Anger is simply another way of deflecting the pain, holding it off, fighting back at it. But the pain of loss is unrelenting. It stalks and chases until it catches us. It is as persistent as wind on the prairies, as constant as cold in the Antarctic, as erosive as a spring flood.[13]

I wonder if that has happened to you. What kind of snapshots have you been holding in your hand? Maybe you have albums full of traumatic loss.

Our expectation is that life will be safe and predictable. We live under the illusion that an impervious bubble surrounds us protecting us from harm. It's always other people that experience trauma, never us, or so we think. When trauma strikes, when our bubble bursts, our world changes.

The loss associated with trauma is the sudden realization that life is not safe and predictable; you have no control. You are vulnerable to the whims of nature and the choices other people make.

What you expected: safety and a predictable life.
What you got: trauma and a story you didn't want to have.
What you lost: safety, control, and predictability.

3. Exposed Weakness

---

[12] Lenore Terr, *Too Scared to Cry; Psychic Trauma in Childhood* (Basic Books), p. 170

[13] Jerry Sittser, *A Grace Disguised*, Expanded Version, (Zondervan), p. 59

In my book, *Healing the Hurts of Your Past*, I talk about how every person experiences a sense of shame. Shame is a feeling of not measuring up. It's the feeling of being excluded from "the group" of our choice. Because we fear exclusion we cover our weaknesses. It might be our weight, education, talent, or a number of things. It's no wonder that we get mad when someone exposes what we've worked so hard to cover up.

A friend of mine is admittedly overweight. He's not proud of it, but he told me that rarely a day goes by when someone doesn't feel the need to remind him of his weight: usually in the form of a sarcastic joke and often in front of other people. It hurts, and as a result he finds himself cutting people out of his life.

Your weaknesses get exposed all the time: when you are a child and you are picked last for your team, when your spouse or friend corrects you in public, or when you are reminded of your past failures. Every exposure hurts, and it ticks you off.

What causes the anger? We trust people to respect us and keep our weaknesses confidential. When they expose our weakness in front of others we lose that trust. It's a betrayal. We might even lose the relationship because of it. And through it all, we lose control of the person exposing us.

What you expected: respect, trust, and privacy.
What you got: exposed weakness, betrayal, and embarrassment.
What you lost: respect, a sense of dignity, control, trust, and relationship.

4. Embarrassing Behavior

The Bible tells a story about King David when he was bringing the Ark of God back to Jerusalem. The Ark was a wooden chest that held the Ten Commandments, but more than that, it was associated with the presence of God. The Ark had been left outside of Jerusalem, and David decided it was time to bring the Ark back to where it belonged.

David was the enthusiastic type. He was excited about the Ark coming to Jerusalem, so he started dancing in worship. He must have gotten hot because the Bible says he stripped off his royal robes and only had on his underwear. Then it says:

> When David returned home to bless his household, Michal daughter of Saul came out to meet him and said, "How the king of Israel has distinguished himself today, going around half-naked in full view of the slave girls of his servants as any vulgar fellow would!"   2 Samuel 6:20

Michal was David's wife. David embarrassed her. She expected him to act dignified. After all, he was the king. She expected him to honor her as his wife, but when David danced half-naked in front of the slave girls, Michal lost her honor. It was guilt by association.

Have you ever felt that way...someone close to you did something in public that was a bad reflection on you? I get flashbacks to high school when some of my friends would do stupid things in public. There you are, stuck with Bozo the Clown, and no way out. It's not only a loss of your public image but also a loss of control. You can't do anything about it. Their actions make you look bad, and you have to sit there and take it. That's something that will tick you off!

What you expected: respect, good image, and reputation.
What you got: embarrassing behavior.
What you lost: sense of dignity, respect, image, control, and relationships.

5. Irritating Behavior

I may be one of the few people in the world who actually likes waiting in airports. I don't even mind if the flight gets delayed because that means I have more time to sit and read at my leisure. At least, I used to like to wait in airports. That was before cell phones. Now, when I wait for my flight, I'm surrounded by people who include me in their personal conversations. It's like being stuck in a phone booth with three other people! My expectation is that I'll have some peace and quiet waiting for my plane, almost like sitting in a library, but my reality is far from that. It ticks me off!

Cell phones are just one of hundreds of things that tick us off. We all have our pet peeves. Maybe it's the woman at work who talks when she should be working or your friend's cigarette smoke or their gum chewing. Maybe it's how your kids never pick up their rooms or play their music too loud. It might be how your husband always changes channels when you try to watch a show. The list goes on and on. The offending behavior may not be morally wrong, it just ticks you off.

Sometimes we'll tell our friends or family members that we are irritated by their behavior, and they push back saying: *What's the big deal? So what if I was fifteen minutes late?* Your response is typically to feel guilty, after all, fifteen minutes isn't a big deal. But if you were quick on your feet you could explain to them what hurts isn't the fifteen minutes (the primary loss) as much as how you feel disrespected by them when they fail to call to tell you they'll be late (the secondary loss).

What you expected: peace and quiet, focus, and respect.
What you got: irritating behavior.
What you lost: peace, quiet, control, focus, and respect.

6. Limited Choices

We live in a world of options. Options aren't decreasing; they are increasing every day. Speaking of cell phones, have you picked out a service plan lately? Chosen a new phone? There are so many options it will make your head spin. Our culture has trained us to expect choice, so when our choices are limited, we experience a loss and often get angry: *What? I thought this phone had 200,000 apps and there are only 150,000? What a rip off!*

I see this in the drug treatment program where I consult. Clients come into the program and are immediately told when they will get up, when they will eat, what they will eat, when they can or can't have a cigarette, and when they'll go to bed. They can't even take an aspirin without permission. Do you think they get angry? You bet they do! About once a month there is an all-out meltdown. Everyone's anger peaks at the same time and look out! That's when I'm glad I'm just a consultant! The staff gets to talk them down.

Why do we react so strongly to limited choices? Are we just selfish and want our way? Again, it goes deeper than that. It has to do with how

God made us. The ability to choose is intrinsic to our humanity. Reasoned choice is one of the many qualities that make us like God. We enjoy the ability to choose. It gives us a sense of power, control, and a sense of identity. When you restrict someone's ability to choose they can easily experience a loss and become angry. They see it as an injustice.

Theologian and author, Dallas Willard writes:
> In creating human beings God made them to rule, to reign, to have dominion in a limited sphere. Only so can they be persons. Any being that has say over nothing at all is no person... They would be reduced to completely passive observers who count for nothing, who make no difference.[14]

Willard tells us that when we don't have say or choice in matters, we feel insignificant. We feel like less of a person and naturally get angry. For example, the first time I visited a jail I was shocked at how prisoners were treated. They were led around and told what to do as if they had no mind or ability to think on their own. They were given no choice. Everything was predetermined for them. I understand that jail has its limitations, but if we want to rehabilitate people we should find a way to affirm the prisoner's sense of dignity. Otherwise, it will be too easy for them to give up on themselves and return to a lifestyle that matches their self-concept.

Our local food pantry grasped this idea when they changed their procedure for food distribution. In the past, when people came to the pantry, a volunteer would give the customers a preselected bag of food and send them on their way. As the staff reflected on this experience, they felt it was demeaning. So the food pantry was redesigned to look like a mini-grocery store, and people are now given carts. They are free to go through the warehouse and choose what they want. This new freedom has given them unlimited choice and as a result, a renewed sense of dignity.

What are some of the ways that your choices are limited? A common

---

[14] Dallas Willard, *The Divine Conspiracy*, (HarperOne), p. 21

way is when someone makes a decision without asking for your input. Maybe your spouse goes out and buys a big-ticket item: a big screen TV or even a car. Or how about when someone speaks for you? They put words in your mouth: words you didn't choose. Or think of the elderly. Their choices are limited every day as they slowly lose their hearing, mobility, and health. I saw this in the residents that lived in my mother's senior care home. I often observed a baseline of anger in people as they grew tired of their aging bodies. Or finally, when your spouse walks out after thirty years of marriage. If you are left with no income or insurance, these limitations can make your retirement years a nightmare. Anytime someone else's choice significantly limits your life in a negative way you'll get mad.

What you expected: freedom to choose, options
What you got: limited choices
What you lost: control, sense of dignity, independence, freedom, options

7. Unmet Needs

When I was a boy there was one kind of athletic shoe. We called everything a "tennis shoe" and we used it for tennis, basketball, track, soccer, and running. When my oldest daughter started playing sports, we bought her a pair of shoes for basketball. Then soccer season came along, and she wanted soccer shoes. *What? Didn't we just buy her a good pair of shoes?* I was all ready to launch into my "Back in my day..." speech when my wife thankfully intervened. You can't play soccer in basketball shoes. Disaster averted.

That scenario plays out in hundreds of homes every day. Children ask for what they "need" (sometimes accurate and sometimes not), and parents dismiss the need as unnecessary. It often ends in anger: sometimes tantrums, or outright rebellion.

When your needs aren't met it's easy to feel rejected. It's demeaning to have to ask for something only to have someone refuse. It communicates you aren't worthy to have your needs met. The message we "hear" is: *If you were important, I'd meet your needs, but you're not. So I won't.* That will tick you off...*every time*.

At one of my early jobs, I had a salary way below the standard for the industry. I was desperate for income, so I took the job. Any salary was better than no salary, but it didn't take long for me to realize that I couldn't live on that salary; so I brought it to the attention of the company. They said they hoped to address it sometime in the coming year. I was not happy, but I only got madder as the year dragged on with no change. I had to bring it up again and again. Finally they gave me a raise, but it was too late. I already heard them loud and clear: *Your needs aren't that important.* As soon as I was able to change jobs, I did.

What you expected: needs met.
What you got: nothing.
What you lost: respect, sense of dignity, control, compassion.

These are seven triggers that can tick us off: seven types of loss that provoke us to anger. Can you relate?

Write it down:
- *Which of the seven triggers stand out to you?*

- *Do they share any common theme?*

The Ah-Ha Moment
As you read through this section did you see any recurring losses? The two words that kept coming up are "respect" and "control". Losing respect and control are at the root of 90% of our anger. This was the "ah-ha" moment that I talked about at the beginning of the chapter. I was surprised to see this. It actually gave me some hope. If I could only discover how to deal with these two losses, then I might well be on my way to resolving my anger issues and helping others as well. I'll look at our need for respect and control in the next chapter.

Chapter Nine:

Anger, Respect & Control

If I want to shake you up and get in your head all I have to do is disrespect you or threaten your sense of control. Nothing undoes you quicker.

What can you do to prevent this from happening? Thankfully, the Bible shows us.

Respect
The biblical approach to respect is radical. Both Jesus and the apostle Paul said we must die to our need for it. Jesus put it this way:
> Whoever wants to be my disciple must deny themselves and take up their cross and follow me. Matthew 16:24

Paul followed with an example of what it means to deny himself:
> I have been crucified with Christ and I no longer live, but

> Christ lives in me. The life I now live in the body, I live by faith in the Son of God, who loved me and gave himself for me. Galatians 2:20

In other words, he made a fundamental shift in where he looked for life, strength, and validation. He died to life "as we know it" and trusted fully in the life that God brings from within. What does that have to do with respect? Everything. You can die to your need for everyone to like you, pat you on the back, and tell you how valuable you are. That only leads to disappointment, hurt, and anger when it doesn't happen. It's better to look inwardly to find your worth and acceptance from God.

The Bible takes just twenty-seven verses to communicate our value. *Twenty-seven verses.* God gets right to the point. He knows how deep our need is to be validated. It says:
> God created man in his own image, in the image of God he created him; male and female he created them. Genesis 1:27

Need I say any more? You've been created in God's image. It doesn't matter how many nicks and stains you have. Beneath it all lays the image of God.

What this means is that your value doesn't come from your daily performance. God confers it on you. It's a gift. It's unconditional. You can't earn it, and you can't lose it. Once you believe this and let it sink into the depths of your soul, you will be FEARLESS. You realize that no one can take your value away, and no foolishness on your part can negate it.

When people offer you respect, consider it a bonus rather than a necessity. If they disrespect you, it shouldn't take anything away from your self-worth. For example, if someone puts you down, it's much easier to separate yourself from the criticism if you are convinced that God sees you having infinite worth. The criticism might still hurt, but it doesn't have to devastate you. You can keep your head up, brush yourself off, and move on without responding in anger. The Bible says:
> Let God be true and every man a liar! Romans 3:4

Absolutely. Listen to what *God* says about your value. People will lie to you about your worth. Even *you* will lie about your worth, but God is true. Listen to him, and you will be less likely to get stuck in anger.

Write it down:

- *Is it hard to die to your need for affirmation?*

- *Who do you look to most for affirmation?*

- *Who most often lets you down in this regard?*

- Consider memorizing Bible verses that affirm your worth so you can quote them to yourself the next time you are invalidated. Note: I offer forty verses like this in the back of my book, *Healing the Hurts of Your Past*.

Control

The Bible also addresses your loss of control by assuring you that God is in control.

> Do not fear, for I am with you; do not be dismayed, for I am your God. I will strengthen you and help you; I will uphold you with my righteous right hand. Isaiah 41:10

> Even though I walk through the valley of the shadow of death, I will fear no evil, for you are with me; your rod and your staff, they comfort me. Psalm 23:4

Admittedly, it doesn't always look like God is in control. That's why it's a matter of faith. If you can trust what the Bible says, you can turn your fear of losing control over to him. For example, imagine I walk into work tomorrow and get fired. It would be a huge loss. My tendency would be to react in anger. I'd feel cut off: adrift. I'd fill with fear and anger at the inevitable string of losses that I'd be convinced would come my way.

But what if I stopped myself and said, *Wait a minute. God was not surprised by this event. I am not in control; He is. I won't fear. I won't get mad. I'll wait and trust that something good will come out of this. I'm not stuck. My options, in God, are limitless.*

Faith Transforms The Moment

You don't have to get ticked off if you let your faith in God impact the losses of respect and control. Your faith can transform your experience and free you to see things in a new way.

Our mistake, in situations like these, is that we focus on the primary loss. We think that if our offender will just stop doing it (whatever "it" is) everything will be okay. Or sometimes we think yelling louder will get "it" to stop. If we can't get "it" to stop then we might resort to avoiding our offender or numbing ourselves (i.e. alcohol, video games, etc.) just to ease the pain.

You may not realize it, but these are all tactics that we use to gain back control. These tactics get you stuck...and *keep* you stuck. If you want to change your situation, it has less to do with changing your offender and more to do with changing you. You need to go deeper in your understanding of your anger and address the underlying secondary issues. Bring your anger to God with a prayer like this:

> *God...I've been thinking about my anger, and I realize that it's not so much about this isolated problem in front of me. It's more about my feeling disrespected. It's more about me not having control. Before I say anything to this person, what do You want to say to me? What do I need to know about my insecurities and fear? Help me see this from Your perspective.*

If you listen closely, you might hear God say something like this:
> *You are right. You aren't in control.*
> *I am. Trust me.*
> *You HAVE been disrespected. I know it hurts.*
> *My respect is all that really matters.*
> *Don't retaliate, but don't run away either. Engage.*
> *Be smart. Be constructive.*
> *Tell them how you feel: respectfully and with a resolve to restore, not attack.*

*And be patient. LISTEN. Don't force it.
Let ME do MY work in MY way in MY time.*

Anger is tricky business. It can be intimidating, but don't let it get you stuck. The Bible tells us that if we lack wisdom we should ask God for it, and he will give us a wealth of wisdom (see James 1:5). I hope you'll try that. What have you got to lose?

An Example For Us

Dr. Martin Luther King Jr. exemplified what I'm talking about here in regard to respect and control. Back in the 1960's King was angry with a number of things in the United States. He was angry that blacks were invalidated. He was angry that their choices were limited and that they had unmet needs. He took his anger to God, and God gave him a radical idea: non-violent protests. He said:

> Nonviolence means avoiding not only external physical violence, but also internal violence of spirit. You not only refuse to shoot a man, but you refuse to hate him.

King was willing to trust God for the respect and control that was so desperately needed. That was not normal thinking. A lot of blacks didn't like the idea. They felt it was passive. They didn't want to wait to gain control or respect; they wanted it now. Isn't that how we often respond? But King's approach changed our nation. It might change you too.

Write it down:

- *How much do you think losing control impacts your anger?*

- *Consider memorizing scripture that will remind you of God's control for the moments you feel you've lost control.*

Chapter Ten:

Stuck in Infectious Attitudes

Years ago my oldest daughter had a grade school teacher who died from an infection. It began with a pimple on her leg. Then it got infected. Seemingly harmless, right? The infection entered her bloodstream, and when it hit the bloodstream the infection circulated to every organ in her body. One organ after another shut down, until it finally killed her.

Infections are like that. They start small and look harmless, but if they aren't treated

quickly, they can be deadly.

I wonder if you've let your anger become infectious. Untreated anger doesn't fade away (as people often think when they say, "Time heals all wounds.") Untreated anger leads to resentment. Resentment leads to bitterness. Bitterness leads to hatred, and it only gets worse from there. Like cement setting around your feet, anger holds you in place while resentment, bitterness, and hatred invade your heart. These attitudes change who you are and how you live your life.

> In her book, *Forgiving the Unforgivable*, Beverly Flanigan says:
> Unforgiveness is like an abscess inside you that just grows and grows. And then it affects all the other things that you touch.[15]

We don't want to believe that about our anger: that it affects everything we touch. We like to think we can isolate and compartmentalize it: targeting our anger to only land on the person or object of our anger with no splash back, that is, without any negative consequences, but that's delusional. There is always splash back. Anger impacts you and every relationship you have in a variety of negative ways.

We rarely see it happening. The infection starts small and slowly takes over. So let me give you some warning signs. Following are some of the infectious attitudes that develop when your anger goes untreated. See if any of these sound familiar and, if so, take corrective action.

Self-righteousness: When someone offends you it's easy to think you'd never do what he or she did. You are above that. You forget about all the times either you've done the same thing or at least considered it. The more evil you paint your offender, the better you feel about yourself.

Criticalness: When you are offended the easiest recourse is to strike back with words. Your offender can't do anything right. Your words serve as a barrier to keep your offender from getting close enough to hurt you again. It's amazing to hear the words that flow from a

---

[15] Beverly Flanigan, *Forgiving the Unforgivable: Overcoming the Bitter Legacy of Intimate Wounds*, (Wiley Press) p. 143

wounded person's mouth. The Bible says:

> The tongue is ...a fire, a world of evil among the parts of the body. It corrupts the whole person, sets the whole course of one's life on fire, and is itself set on fire by hell. It is a restless evil, full of deadly poison. With our tongue we praise our Lord and Father, and with it we curse human beings, who have been made in God's likeness. James 3:6-9

Pessimism: Unresolved anger turns you into a negative person. When you believe you got a raw deal, you start to think life is unfair altogether. You develop a chip on your shoulder you don't even know exists but is obvious to everyone else.

Psychologists talk about the three P's of pessimism: *personal, pervasive*, and *permanent*. In other words, pessimists take everything personally. The problem is all about them. It's pervasive, meaning that the problem affects every aspect of their life. And it's permanent; things will never change. Life will always be bad.

Withdrawing: When life is unfair, you want to do what you can to avoid being hurt again. Withdrawing only makes sense. You slowly become less and less engaged. As you do, your friends get the message and stop including you. Before you know it, you are alone. You blame your friends for abandoning you. Sadly, you don't see what you've done.

Self-pity: Self-pity is an emotional backwater, meaning: it's an easy place to get stuck. Self-pity results when you believe your situation is permanent and untreatable. There's nothing you can do to change your lot in life so, rather than accept your situation and move on, you settle for feeling sorry for yourself and let others do the same. You prefer sympathy over changing your outlook.

Entitlement: Entitlement causes you to use your offense to justify doing what you want, even if it's immoral or illegal. If you are passed over for a promotion, you might feel justified in stealing from your company because "you deserve it." If you are an alcoholic, you might feel justified in drinking because your spouse rejected you. If you are addicted to porn, you might pick a fight with your wife as an excuse to turn to your porn sites. Entitlement is a cheap excuse to do what you want without taking responsibility for it.

Rage: Part of feeling entitled is allowing yourself to vent your anger inappropriately. Rage is like that. You justify it because what was done to you seems so wrong. You believe you can suspend normal protocol and cut loose. You know it's not right, but you allow yourself to lose control because it feels good, and you think you deserve this guilty pleasure. Plus it often brings a level of control as people cower in front of you. Over time, you become addicted to the rush and power that rage offers.

Wishing Harm: You may never admit it, but you wouldn't mind seeing your offender get sick, hurt, or even die. You wouldn't do anything to cause harm directly, but you'd like to see your offender suffer a little for what they've done to you. And if they die, well…maybe they deserve it.

Revenge: Revenge goes beyond wishing harm and takes vengeance into your own hands. You don't want to forgive. You want payback. Lewis Smedes tells us what's wrong with revenge. He says:

> The problem with revenge is that it never gets what it wants; it never evens the score. Fairness never comes. The chain reaction set off by every act of vengeance always takes its unhindered course. It ties both the injured and the injurer to an escalator of pain. Both are stuck on the escalator as long as parity is demanded, and the escalator never stops, never lets anyone off.[16]

Smedes reference to an "escalator of pain" reminds me of the movie *Changing Lanes* with Samuel Jackson and Ben Affleck.[17] The movie is about two men involved in a fender-bender in morning rush hour traffic. The entire movie describes an escalator effect between the two where they keep upping the ante of their anger and retaliation. They both have momentary "lapses" where they consider forgiveness, but the other person retaliates and sucks them both back into the fray.

It's a great morality lesson on the danger of trying to achieve payback.

---

[16] *Forgive and Forget*, (Harper One), p. 168
[17] Paramount Pictures, 2002

I had to laugh at what one man said to me after I talked about the dangers of revenge. He asked, "Does that include good revenge?" I had never heard the term "good revenge" before, so I asked him what he meant. He explained he worked in a detail shop where they clean and buff cars. Their premium package includes a double buffing. He said that if his team doesn't like the car owner they only buff the car once but charge him the same price because he wouldn't know the difference. It was "good" revenge in his mind because it supposedly didn't hurt the offender but satisfied the victim. I assured this man there is no such thing as good revenge, but after thinking about it, I realized that I had engaged in "good revenge" myself through the years.

Write it down:

- Think about these attitudes: self-righteous, critical, pessimistic, self-pitying, entitled, withdrawing, raging, wishing harm, and seeking revenge. *Which of these words describe you? Is that who you want to be?*

- *Are you willing to do what it takes to recover from this infection?*

- *Have you ever engaged in "good revenge"?*

Warning

Let me warn you, if you let your wound go untreated, if you choose to remain stuck; you may find your life becomes *defined* by the offense. You *become* the offense. It is your focal point in life. It dominates your thinking, your conversation, and your reason for living. It becomes an idol to you, taking the place of God. Again, Beverly Flanigan says:

> [anger]...that has festered and grown is like a worm crawling into an apple. It can take hold of your core and damage the heart permanently... If [a person] is allowed to damage your core, you have let someone else not only destroy your dreams but destroy you. That is too high a price to pay for anything. It is one thing to have your heart broken; it is quite another to have it poisoned. Broken hearts repair. Poisoned hearts

shrivel and die.[18]

The Bible gives us this charge:
> Make peace with everyone…and see to it…that no bitter root grows up to cause trouble and defile many. Hebrews 12:14,15

The word "defile" here means "to dye or stain, to pollute, contaminate." When you choose to hold onto your anger, you choose to contaminate people with your bitterness. Is that what you want to happen?

Let me pray that you will be able to move on from your hurt and make peace with everyone:
> *Father, I pray for the person reading this today. Help them to see how unresolved anger affects them like a cancer. Show them the infectious attitudes that might be theirs. And help them to see how You are ready and willing to empower them to release their anger so they might make peace with everyone and move on with their life. Amen.*

---

[18] *Forgiving the Unforgivable*, p. 144

Chapter Eleven:

Stuck in Denial

Melanie is the first person at church and the last one to leave. She volunteers every opportunity she gets and participates in two Bible studies every week. Between church and her kids' school activities, she keeps busy. That's the way she likes it because when she slows down long enough to be quiet, she doesn't like what she sees.

Melanie hates her life. Her husband is emotionally disconnected. She fears he's having an affair. Neither of her kids is doing well in school, and she wonders if they'd improve if she were a better mom. Church activities and shuttling her kids to events take the pain away but only for the moment. Melanie is stuck in denial.

Many of us stay stuck because we don't want to admit our situation.

We are embarrassed. We don't think our failures should be a part of our story. We hope by ignoring the bad it will go away: one day we will wake up, and it will just be gone. The nightmare will be over.

But if you never claim the dark side of your story, you can never move on from it. It's like the proverbial elephant in the living room or the emperor with no clothes. Who wants either of them to be a part of their story? No one, but the elephant and the naked guy aren't going anywhere unless you first embrace them as part of your story. When you embrace them you can finally deal with them and get them out of your house!

Let me introduce you to your subconscious mind. It works at minimizing and denying anything painful. It's almost like an inner person taking care of you, making sure you don't get more than your conscious mind can handle. If you have anger issues, which you either don't know how to deal with or have *chosen not* to deal with, your brain volunteers a solution. It's called denial.

An Emotional Shock-Absorber

Denial separates you from the pain of your world. It's a natural "shock-absorber" God gives you to regroup from emotional trauma, somewhat like what your body does by going into shock after *physical* trauma.

Think about the first words out of your mouth when you hear about a tragedy. When my mom called to tell me my father died, the first word out of my mouth was "No!" Now, I knew my dad was dying. I expected the call sooner or later. So why would I say that? It's almost like my mouth gave voice to my subconscious. My conscious mind knew that my mom wasn't lying and that my dad had died, but something deep within me didn't want it to be true and objected by saying "No!"

Denial is initially a good thing. It creates a buffer zone to transition to a new reality, but denial becomes a bad thing if you choose to stay in that place. I like to compare it to living in a rest area. Imagine I'm traveling from Minneapolis to Chicago. I get half way there, and I decide to pull into a rest area. When I get there, it's so nice I decide to pitch a tent and spend the night.

What's really great about the rest area is they have a nice selection of inexpensive food in the vending machines. I can eat and sleep without having to leave the parking lot. I like it so much I decide to spend a second night and then a third. Days turn into weeks and weeks into months. I never make it to Chicago because I end up living at the rest area, totally forgetting why I ever wanted to go to Chicago in the first place.

That sounds silly, but I wonder if that's what you are doing in your life? You aren't getting to where you are supposed to be because living in denial is much more comfortable: less threatening.

John Trent, in his book, *Choosing to Live the Blessing,* says:
> Denial is a form of anesthesia. Sometimes denial is cloaked in self-confident assertions like "I've gone forward with my life" or "I've put the past behind me." But the problem with the past is that it never stays there. It has ways – sometimes subtle, sometimes intrusive – of resurfacing and wreaking havoc on the present. That is why some people seem stuck in a cycle of picking the wrong relationships, making the same mistakes, repeating the same patterns of self-destructive behavior. What they are really stuck in is the past. And they can't go forward until they go back there and begin dealing with some of those painful pictures.[19]

Following is a list of ways denial might be keeping you stuck in your past.

1. Suppression

Have you ever held a beach ball under water? It's hard, but you can do it. You are suppressing it. You can do the same thing with your anger. You purposely choose to "not go there": intentionally pushing down thoughts and feelings about how you've been offended. This is what Trent was talking about when he said we say things like, "I've gone forward with my life" *or* "I've put the past behind me." People often tell me they've forgiven their offender when they really haven't. They've said the words, but in reality they still hold onto their anger. Or they

---

[19] John Trent, *Choosing to Live the Blessing* (WaterBrook Press), p.46

might make a joke about some offense, making light of it, when in reality, it hurt a lot.

People often suppress their anger by forgiving prematurely. By prematurely, I mean they go through the motions of forgiveness: they say the right things, but their heart isn't in it. They haven't really dealt with the loss. Their pseudo-forgiveness makes them think they've dealt with their anger when they haven't.

This is especially true in faith communities that value forgiveness. Their words get ahead of their heart, and their forgiveness comes across as hollow. It's ironic this kind of "forgiveness" can actually be what causes you to stay stuck. You think you've forgiven when, in fact, you haven't. This faux forgiveness is used to help you avoid facing your anger.

I regularly try to slow people down in the forgiveness process. I encourage them to pull up their feelings, explore them, and own them, before they forgive. This is all a part of the process.

2. Displacement

You've heard of people who come home after a bad day at work and kick their dog, yell at their spouse, and slam doors. Rather than addressing the source of their anger, these people deny that it exists. They transfer their anger toward something or someone other than their offender. They don't deny they are angry. They deny the true source of their anger because it's easier to be mad at the dog than deal with the invalidation from their boss or the powerlessness of having a daughter arrested for drugs.

I've seen this in church. Occasionally someone will get mad about some small matter in the church, but then it gets blown out of proportion. I've learned whenever this happens there is usually something going on in their life that is stressing them out. They aren't able to confront the big problem at home, so they confront small problems outside the home.

3. Medication

The cheapest and quickest way to deny your pain is to numb it.

Painkillers, alcohol, and drugs (legal and illegal) all work within a matter of minutes. It's easier to medicate your anger than learn to forgive. That's why some have said that drugs and alcohol are not the problem. They are the *solution*: they solve the pain in the moment. Of course this "solution" brings with it a whole slew of problems, but that's tomorrow. It solves the problem today.

4. Distractions

If you want to go the socially acceptable route to denial, then just get busy with a variety of distractions like work, hobbies, or exercising. That's what Melanie did in my opening example. You get all kinds of affirmation from your friends when in reality you are trying to cover up your pain. You can add a number of different distractions to this list like shopping, eating, vacationing, Facebook, playing video games, or even sleeping.

I have often felt sorry for the bad rap alcoholics get in comparison to these socially acceptable addicts. Alcoholics bear a stigma in our culture that makes them look weak, but in reality, we all turn to some kind of behavior to treat our pain.

5. Caretaking

Caretaking is when you take care of the pain of others so you don't have to look at your own pain. It helps you in a couple of ways; first, it takes your mind off your problem; second, it makes you feel good about helping someone else. Plus, caretaking often gives you all kinds of positive affirmation from other people. You look like the good guy. No one knows your true motivation is to escape the reality of your story.

6. Projection

Have you ever known someone who had a behavioral problem, but they could never see it? Whenever someone tried to point it out they got defensive and pushed back. The amazing thing is they could see the same problem in someone else, whether it was really there or not. You want to say to these people, "If you could only see that clearly when you look in the mirror!" This kind of person projects their problem on others. It's too much for them to admit, so they process their problem by seeing it in others.

7. Over-Spiritualizing

I was teaching this material in a workshop once, and a man raised his hand to ask a question. But it really wasn't a question. He launched into a detailed, circuitous monologue quoting a variety of Bible verses...basically excusing himself from having to face his pain. It was obvious by the looks on the faces of the other attendees they knew what he was doing, but he was clueless. He had all the pieces together in his mind that were necessary to justify his denial, using God and the Bible to do it. By over-spiritualizing his problems he was not only able to deny they existed but feel superior as well.

I differentiate being religious from being truly spiritual. A religious person is happy to hide behind their religion by over-spiritualizing. It makes them look virtuous. At least, that's what they think. Most people can sense the hypocrisy, but a truly spiritual person is a seeker. They go wherever the truth leads them even if that's out of their comfort zone.

Compassion For Those In Denial

It's frustrating to encounter someone in denial. What they do is obviously wrong, but when you understand they are desperately trying to avoid the pain in their life, it's easier to have compassion for them. They are not purposefully being deceptive. They simply turn to the quickest and easiest solution to stop their pain.

I used to live on a farm a few years back. I'd go deep into our woods to cut down trees for firewood. I'd only carry a few things with me: a chainsaw, gas, oil, a few tools, and a rag to wipe the blade off. I was never hurt, but imagine I cut myself out there with the saw. I'm bleeding badly, and I'm scared. Given what I had with me, what might I do to stop the bleeding? I'd probably grab the rag and shove it in the cut, right? I'd grab what worked, what was most available, but could actually kill me if the wound got infected. If I wasn't so scared maybe I'd think to take off my shirt and use it, but in the pressure of the moment I choose a solution that actually creates more problems for me.

That's what many people do when they deny their anger. They use what works in the moment, even though it hurts them in the long run.

Write it down:
- Look through this list of denial. Circle the ones that describe you.

- *What is it that you are trying to cover up?*

- *Has denial kept you stuck in the past?*

The hard part about giving up your denial is that you are immediately struck by what you've been trying to cover up for so long – and that is PAIN. Take away your denial, and the pain is right there staring you in the face.

If you want to find true healing and not just a temporary fix, then addressing your anger, not denying it, is what needs to happen. It's like a physical wound. You can make it feel better by putting ointment on it and bandaging it up. But if you don't clean out the wound first you'll only incubate an infection. Do the hard thing first: clean out the wound, and let the healing begin.

Breaking Through Denial

How do you break through denial? Here are a few things that might help.

1. Be Honest

We often know we are in denial, but as long as people let us get away with it, we keep it up. We allow people to enable us and then justify it by saying, "But all my friends agree with me." That's only because you played them. You manipulated them to agree and not confront you.

Admit to God the charade you've been working so hard to keep in place.

Then tell someone what you've been doing. This is the beginning of getting unstuck.

2. Ask God To Reveal What's Hidden

Sometimes we know we are in denial. Other times we have no idea. One of God's favorite prayers from us must be "God, please show me what's wrong. Show me what I haven't yet seen about myself." When that prayer is sincere, God is more than happy to open your eyes to what you haven't previously seen. God knows the first step to change is to admit. He wants to help you see what the problem is so you can address it.

Sometimes God reveals problems slowly, like a gradual unveiling. Other times it might be more "in your face". Each of us has different capacities to handle self-awareness. God might speak to you by bringing a book, a song, or a sermon your way. He might bring a person to confront you or simply arrest you with a thought. When you actively listen to God, it's amazing what you hear.

You can be proactive in your self-discovery with the help of a counselor. I've prayed with many people, asking God to show them their anger, and right there in the moment, God revealed to the person issues that had been hidden for years.

God wants you to see what you've been denying, not to shame you or make your life more complicated. He wants to help you find healing and freedom so you can move on with your life.

3. Get Feedback

Your friends and family see what you don't. Why not ask them to help you see what you can't? They've probably been waiting for an opportunity to tell you. Why not give them an opportunity? I know it's scary. So is going to the doctor when you think something might be wrong. But you have to do it if you want to find healing. It takes courage to ask for input, but it may be the beginning of the change you've been longing to experience.

Don't ask any random person for input. And don't ask people that will only tell you what you want to hear. Ask people who love you and have proven to be safe in regard to personal issues.

4. Take A Psychological Test

I used to work for a company that sold psychological and personality tests. I took just about every test as a part of my job. I learned a lot about myself! Not all good. The tests were an objective reflection of who I was at the time, and they opened my eyes to things I didn't see about myself.

I often give couples the *Taylor-Johnson Temperament Survey* as part of my pre-marital counseling. It tests for a variety of personality traits. One scale gives a reading on hostility. How people answer the questions gives the test a sense of your level of anger. Many people score high on this scale and are surprised to see their score. They had no idea they were carrying so much hidden anger.

Take Action

The point here is to make sure you recognize your natural tendency to deny what's painful so you can take action. The path of least resistance isn't the way to get unstuck.

Chapter Twelve:

Stuck in Grief

Timothy was a dad whose daughter had been raped twenty-five years ago, yet he spoke like it happened yesterday. He knew the guy who did it. In fact, he almost choked him to death but was stopped before he succeeded. Timothy lived with the memory of that event every day and dreamed of getting vengeance every night.

Timothy was stuck in grief.

When you hear the word "grief" what comes to mind? Most people think of the sadness associated with the death of a loved one. The *Five Stages of Grief* were developed in a book about death and dying, [20] but grief is the process that accompanies *any* loss.
Loss comes in many ways:

---

[20] Elisabeth Kubler-Ross, *On Death and Dying*, (Scribner)

- Miscarriage
- Loss of job
- Divorce
- A child moves away from home
- Loss of health, mobility, etc.
- Canceled wedding
- Change of church
- Move to new home
- Death of a pet

Every loss requires grieving. If it's a small loss (lost car keys, the weather ruins your plans, etc.) it hopefully only takes seconds to recover, but you still grieve the loss before you move on.

I want to walk you through the five stages of grief to help you assess your present situation and see if you might be stuck in grief. One thing to keep in mind; these five stages are meant as a helpful model. The stages may not define your experience, and they do not necessarily go in order.

Stage One: Denial

Denial is a natural reaction to loss as I discussed in the last chapter. In fact, your subconscious mind wants you to stay in denial because it wants to protect you from the pain of what happened.

Denial is to the mind what shock is to the body after it experiences trauma. Both are necessary, but you can't remain in either condition for long and remain healthy. Some people choose to stay in denial long after they should. They tell themselves the loss didn't happen, or the loss wasn't significant. Many people will use addictive habits like drinking, taking drugs, or other excessive behavior to deny their feelings. It's all meant to keep them from feeling the full weight of the loss and taking responsibility for the new life the loss requires.

Stage Two: Anger

When you come out of denial, anger is waiting for you. It hasn't gone anywhere. Anger is the emotional response to loss. It's not bad, but it can be intimidating. It can make you feel like you are losing control.

Some people find it easier to live in denial than deal with the anger over their loss. This reality is what often drives people right back into denial or moves them to the next phase.

Stage Three: Bargaining

Bargaining is where you look for a quick fix. You hope some slick negotiating on your part will avert disaster. You say things to God like, "If you take this problem away I'll go to Africa for life and feed the poor." If your significant-other wants to break up with you, or your spouse wants a divorce, you might plead with them to take you back promising you'll "do anything" to make them happy even though you know the relationship is over.

I see bargaining when people get in a financial mess and try to solve it with a "get-rich-quick" scheme stapled on a bulletin board or advertised on cable TV. Or they might take out a loan to pay off another loan or even resort to theft, selling drugs, or prostitution. In their mind they are "just going to do this once" to solve the loss.

I also see bargaining when people come to church and hope that one church experience, one counseling session, or one pastoral prayer will magically solve their problem like a spiritual "wand" waved over their head, but it doesn't work that way. When that reality sets in, people either go back to denial, get angry again, or move to the next stage.

Stage Four: Depression

This is where some people get stuck for years. It's my opinion that many people on anti-depressants are in this phase of the grief cycle and don't know it. They've experienced some kind of loss and haven't gotten over it. I don't have anything against medication, but I do wonder how many people are medicating a condition they could actually resolve by moving through the grief cycle and not depending on drugs to numb their feelings.

One of the factors keeping people stuck in this phase of grief believes a particular lie. The lie is this:
My life will never be good again.

The loss may have been the death of a loved one, the loss of a job, or something that seems irretrievable to the person. In their mind life will never be the same, and since it can't be the same, then life can never be good.

For example, I love my wife Lisa very much. We have been married for over 30 years and have a great relationship. If she dies before I do, it would be tempting for me to think my life will never be good again. After all, I've been married more years than I've been single and she adds significant joy to my life. It makes sense, but that's a lie.

The truth is my life will never be *the same* again, but that does NOT mean it won't be as good, if not better, than it was before. God isn't limited in bringing me joy and purpose through Lisa alone. Lisa is *one way* God has brought me joy. There are other ways. I have to believe that. If I don't, I am condemning myself to limp through life as half a person stuck in grief should she die before me.

This lie, that life will never be good again, stems from what is often called a *poverty mentality*. A poverty mentality is when people believe there is only one "pie," so to speak, and when the pie is gone you are out of luck. There is nothing left. The poverty mentality would look at my life and say, "Remy, look at the things that make up your life. This is as good as it gets. Don't lose anything because when they are gone you'll never see them again. It can only get worse from here on out." As I incur loss after loss in life my world gets smaller and smaller.

The opposite of a poverty mentality is an abundance mentality. An abundance mentality believes that God is always making new pies. The abundance mentality would say, "Remy, in life things come and go. There will be losses, but just remember; whenever you lose something, there is always more from where that came from. You never have to go without."

This is where a belief in God is so important to getting unstuck. If what you see in life is all you get and there is no God to add to your life after your loss, then yes, that is depressing. But if God exists and he loves you, then no loss is insurmountable. There may be setbacks, but there will be no defeats. Your life may not be the same as before, but it can still be good.

Stage Five: Acceptance

God has the power to make your life good again, but you have to look for it. It requires working at getting a fresh perspective. Some people insist on staying in the past: dwelling on what was. If they were offended, they might pursue their offender relentlessly or anyone associated with their loss. Instead of asking God to help them achieve acceptance, they dog their offender, insisting they make things right. Or if not the offender, then maybe some person associated with the loss: a doctor, police officer, teacher, family member, etc. They think happiness will come only when they can convince someone to "fix" their problem for them. Again, this results from a poverty mentality. If you are convinced that every loss robs you of life then you will fight to recapture any loss.

Isn't this attitude what causes us to lie awake for endless hours rehashing the events that led up to the loss? We believe if we rethink it one more time, we will solve the loss. But the truth is that we will only be happy when we can let the issue die and release everyone from the weight of fixing our loss. As long as we insist someone out there can do something to "make it all better" we remain stuck.

No Short Cut

There is no short cut to reaching the acceptance phase. I wish there was. The reason we default to denial is because of the pain that goes along with grieving. But grieving is what we must do. Accept the loss. Feel the full weight of it: the pain of it. Give yourself permission to feel every emotion that comes your way: sadness, anger, and fear. Embrace them. These emotions often scare people. They are afraid where they might take them. It might feel like it's too much, like they will crush you, like you can't take it, but you can. You must, if you want to reclaim your life and move on.

Just remember, grief is a phase: a season. It will pass. Like a tide, it will come in and go out. There is a price to pay for stopping the process. You must move through the entire grief process if you want to reclaim your life. There must be a death and burial before the resurrection. Be willing to experience the loneliness and confusion that comes as you reorient your life to exist without whatever or whomever it was you lost. God will bring you through to the other side if you let him.

Faith And Grief

Some people have the misunderstanding that if you have faith in God you shouldn't grieve. If you really trust God then you just move on without missing a step. That is foolish. God wired us to have deep connections. Grief is a sign of our investment in life. To move on after a loss without missing a beat tells me there is something wrong. Either there was no true connection between you and the person in the first place or you are denying your feelings. It is unfair of you to not allow yourself to grieve. If people close to you won't allow you to grieve, then you should create some distance between you and them until you have a chance to grieve.

My point here is to give you permission to grieve. Our culture doesn't know how to grieve. As a result many live with unresolved issues. We live in an era of sixty-minute television dramas or thirty-minute sermons where everything is resolved in a nice package. Life isn't that neat and tidy. In fact, life is messy. We need to give ourselves the time it takes to grieve.

Having said that, grief is not a place you want to get stuck. It is a place you want to move *through*.

Write it down:

- *What stood out to you most about the stages of grief?*

- *Are there any stages of grief where you are presently stuck?*

- *Do you believe the lie that life will never be good again?*

- *What losses still need grieving in your life? Think back through the stages of life...even as a child.*

Chapter Thirteen:

Seven Factors That Keep You Stuck

Tom came to see me not long ago. He thought I might be a good person to talk to about his daughter who was abusing drugs. Tom was a widower facing this on his own. Life had gotten crazy for him.

His wife died a few years earlier from cancer. When his daughter started using drugs, he confronted her. He thought that was the end of it, but it was only the beginning. Unfortunately she didn't dabble in drugs; she went straight to methamphetamine (or meth). Meth is highly addictive and an epidemic in Wisconsin.

Tom went out of his way to help his daughter but to no avail. After a few scrapes with the law, she ended up in treatment, only to relapse soon after. This became a cycle. The only time Tom's daughter contacted him was to bail her out of jail.

Tom had enough. He decided to try the "tough love" route, welcoming her back home only after she had been straight for six months and willing to abide by house rules. His daughter rejected his offer. She accepted the offer of a nearby relative who had "compassion" for her.

Tom was looking for some sanity. He decided to move to Minnesota to be near friends and start a new life for the rest of his kids. The past years had thrown his family into chaos; his daughter's drama made life hard for her three younger brothers. Tom wanted to create some space by moving, but his decision to move brought the wrath of his wife's family. They resented Tom taking away the few connections they had to their deceased daughter. They regularly questioned Tom's sons, asking them, "How can your dad do this to the family?"

Tom was stuck. People were mad at him. He was mad at them. He came to me to see if I thought his choices were good ones or not. He was ready to move on with his life, but he was afraid that, if he was wrong, moving would only compound his problems. Isn't it sad that there can be so much tension among family members?

Beverly Flanigan says in her book, *Forgiving the Unforgivable*:
> The worst kind of human wounds occur not on battlefields but in our homes. The worst injurers are not enemies or strangers in a foxhole but our husbands and wives, children, parents, and friends. Wherever love has been a part of relationships, the shrapnel of human destruction is strewn in our living rooms and bedrooms in the form of aborted dreams and wounded hopes. Wars may terminate with the signing of peace treaties, but intimate injuries have no such formal mechanisms for ending them. The most intimate of injuries

are often left festering and unresolved – either unforgiven or unforgivable.[21]

Created To Connect

Why is it these injuries cause us so much pain? One of the reasons is because God wired us for connection. When our connections break down, it distorts God's design for us. The Bible quotes God saying, "Let us make mankind in our image" (Genesis 1:26). Then God created Adam and Eve. Note how God refers to himself as "us" and then creates two people in relationship as a reflection of his image. That tells me: *God is relational by nature*. I don't understand it, but the Bible speaks about God as Father, Son, and Spirit being in relationship with each other (what's traditionally referred to as the Trinity).

Since we are created in God's image, we must also be relational by nature. To be in relationship is part of our core identity. To break relationship with people tears the fabric of that identity. It hurts. It creates a tension: a dissonance. It creates disharmony, like an out of tune piano that grates on us.

Disharmony bothers God too. That's why the Bible says God hates divorce (Malachi 2:16). God doesn't just hate marital divorce. He hates any kind of divorce, whether it's between friends, family, or even within a church. The Bible doesn't say God hates *the people* involved in divorce. He hates the breakup of a relationship. That's because divorce is the opposite of who God is and who he created us to be. It's foreign to his character.

God is unity by nature. He created us to reflect that unity. When people see true unity in a marriage, family, or church they get a glimpse of the nature of God. When they see separation and divorce, they see the very opposite of God. That's why reconciliation is so important to God; it restores the beauty of unity and reveals his character to the world.

Since relational unity is part of our spiritual DNA, anything that undermines unity bothers us. That's why we get emotional and lose sleep when our relationships break down.

---

[21] *Forgiving the Unforgivable,* p. 5

I opened this chapter talking about Tom. What do you think he should do? Before I tell you what I told Tom, I want to walk you through seven factors that often cause people to get stuck in their relationships.

Write it down:
- *Think about your anger. How much of it is related to another person?*

- *What is it about these people that make you angry? Why do you think that is?*

- *Are there people you need to move toward to restore unity?*

- *Are there people you need to move away from to protect yourself?*

1. Weak Boundaries

A big reason people get stuck in anger is they have too many intruders in their life: people that either take advantage of them or insist on getting in the middle of their business. This happens when people have no boundaries or at least weak boundaries.

Here's a picture of what I mean by boundaries. Years ago I co-owned a dairy farm. Our house was just inside the west edge of our property line. An old, droopy, barbed wire fence was all that separated us from our neighbors. I liked living there because our neighbor grazed his cows right outside our windows. It was fun watching the cows during the day, and at night I enjoyed falling asleep to the sound of them chewing the grass.

One night I heard their chewing, but it seemed a lot closer than usual. Instead of hearing the cows outside our west window I heard them outside our west, north, and east window, much like "surround sound." I knew something was up, so I jumped out of bed and flipped on the yard light. Sure enough, the cows had pushed through the barbed wire fence and taken advantage of the fresh grass in our yard. They also left some free fertilizer!

This is a perfect example of what happens when you have a weak boundary. People push their way into your life, take what's not theirs, and make a mess! As long as the boundary is respected, everything is fine, even if they are "right outside of your window," so to speak. You feel safe because you know the boundary is observed, but as soon as that boundary is crossed, you experience a loss and anger results.

What Are Boundaries?

A boundary is something you put in place to create personal space. It helps determine who you are and who you are not, or where you stop and another person starts.[22] Boundaries can be emotional or physical. A *physical* boundary could be as simple as liking to have at least one empty seat between you and the next person in a theater. Or it could be more serious than that. Did you ever see the movie, *What About Bob?* That movie is all about crossed boundaries.

Bill Murray plays Bob, a highly insecure patient who can't live without his psychiatrist, Dr. Leo Marvin, played by Richard Dreyfus. Dr. Leo is desperate to find peace in his life, so he retreats to his New England cabin. Bob tracks him down and manages to work his way into his doctor's family vacation, crossing every boundary Dr. Leo puts up. Dr. Leo faces his anger through the whole movie. It's both funny and painful to watch as you imagine someone like Bob crossing your boundaries.

Bob crossed a number of *physical* boundaries, but there are also *emotional* boundaries. I was talking to a young couple recently, and

---

[22] For an excellent study on boundaries read, *Boundaries: When to Say YES, When to Say NO, To Take Control of Your Life* by John Townsend and Henry Cloud (Zondervan)

they told me they have a rule: no phone calls during a meal together. Mealtime is their "personal time," and they don't want anyone entering that space. They wisely laid down an emotional boundary.

Anger Is A Boundary Detector

The interesting thing about boundaries is you don't always know you have them until they are crossed, and you get angry. That's why I call anger a "boundary detector." Your anger alerts you and your offender to the fact a boundary has been crossed.

The reason the young couple above made their rule about no phone-calls was because the husband used to take calls during meals, and his wife often ate alone listening to his one-sided conversations. She found herself getting angry. Thankfully they understood what was happening: their personal space was violated by callers. Once they put the rule in place enforcing the boundary, they were able to reclaim suppertime for themselves.

Many couples are not so perceptive. For this couple, anger actually helped *resolve* their conflict because it helped identify a hidden boundary. Most people don't think of anger as something to resolve conflict, but it *can* if you use it to your advantage. When you see anger in this light, it removes the shame or guilt from experiencing it. It's no longer a bad emotion. It becomes a good emotion that warns you of a crossed boundary.

Communicating Boundaries

When someone provokes you to anger, ask yourself: *What boundary of mine did she cross? What loss am I experiencing?* Once you discover what that is, ask yourself: *Is this person aware of my boundary? Have I ever told her about it?* Too often we assume people should know our boundaries. We assume everyone is like we are, but of course, they are not. It's up to us to communicate our boundaries so others can respect them.

I have a friend who felt stuck in a job he didn't like. He actually liked the job itself, but his boss kept asking him to do more and more work that made him stay late: work not in his job description. He told me he was going to have to quit his job because he didn't like going home late all the time. He felt used and angry. I asked him if he ever told his boss how he felt. He said, "No". I asked, "Why not?" He said he "didn't want to have the awkward conversation," either making his boss look bad or making him sound lazy.

I told him he needed to have the conversation before he quit. My guess was his boss had no clue what he was doing or the negative impact it was having on my friend. Before he quit, he really owed it to his boss, and to himself, to tell his boss how he felt.

This is a classic case of the need to establish boundaries in a relationship. I recommended that my friend ask for a minute of his boss's time and say something like this:

> *I need you to help me understand something. Lately you've asked me to do extra work that has never been a part of my job description. I want to be a team player, but I don't know if you realize how much time these tasks require. I've had to stay late on a regular basis just to get everything done. Is that something you expect from me?*

My friend could ask the question and see what his boss had to say. His boss might be surprised to learn what was happening and reduce his demands. If not, my friend would then have to decide how much he wanted the job. I wanted him to see he had some control in the situation. He wasn't a victim. To simply up and quit without having the conversation was a missed opportunity.

By taking this kind of proactive approach in your relationships, you use your anger to *resolve* conflict. When you define your boundaries, you create personal space between you and the other person in a calm, respectful manner. Instead of *losing* the relationship, you actually have the potential to *improve* it. Hopefully the other person will understand you better and know how to respect your space. It's good for both of you! It's amazing how quickly people will respect your boundaries once they know what they are.

Write it down:

- Think through your relationships. *Are your boundaries too weak, too strong, or just right?*

- List the people that you believe have invaded your space and in what ways. *Does this help you understand why you carry a load of anger? Can you see how you tend to stay stuck when you have so many unwanted people in your life?*

- *Do you think your life would be less stressful if you had healthy boundaries in place?*

- *Have you expected people to know your boundaries even though you've never communicated your boundaries to them?*

- Take your list of boundary breakers, and make it your "to-do" list. These are the people you need to speak to about how they cross your boundaries. You can do it!

2. Shame

Another reason people stay stuck in anger is because anger is magnified by a personal sense of shame. In his book, *The Safest Place on Earth*, Larry Crabb mentions the findings of therapist Irving Yalom:

> Yalom plays the Top Secret game with people in his groups. He asks them to write out the single thing about themselves they are least inclined to share and to then return the paper unsigned. The most frequent top secret is the admission "I feel utterly worthless. No one would want me if they knew me."

I feel utterly worthless. No one would want me if they knew me. Is that how you feel about yourself? These are the feelings of shame. This is why the shamed person is often quick to get angry. Their sense of worthlessness is a major loss to them.

In my first book, *Healing the Hurts of Your Past: a guide to overcoming the pain of shame*, I deal extensively with shame. I talk about five roots of shame:

1. Abuse
2. Ridicule
3. Neglect
4. Family and Personal Secrets
5. Trauma

Each of these can impact you so deeply that you doubt your worth. You not only see yourself as flawed but worthless. You begin to doubt your intrinsic value. Or as I wrote in the book, you believe a variety of lies like: "I don't belong," "I don't deserve it," "I should give up now," "I will never succeed." These lies are at the core of shame. Where there are no lies, there is no shame. Wherever there are lies, there will always be shame.

Because the shame-based person feels as though they fall short of expectations, they live in a constant state of loss. They never "arrive." The "carrot" is always in front of them. Since we know loss evokes anger, you often find shame and anger together. People are angry with *themselves* for falling short, angry with *those who judge them* for falling short, and angry with *God* for making them that way.

In order to get unstuck, it's important to confront your shame.

Write it down:

- *How much do you struggle with a sense of shame?*

- *Do you agree with the statement "I feel utterly worthless; no one would want me if they knew me"?*

- *Do you see how your shame causes anger?*

3. Narcissism

Closely linked to shame is narcissism. Narcissism is defined as having extreme pride in oneself to the point of grandiosity. Because of this extreme self-interest the person is unable to have empathy for others, blocking thoughts of forgiveness. In fact, one researcher calls narcissism "the antithesis of the forgiving personality."[23]

The narcissist isn't concerned for other people but rather sees them as an extension of themselves: as a means to an end. They feel a strong sense of entitlement with the right to exploit others for their personal benefit. When someone fails the narcissist, there is no attempt to reconcile the relationship. They merely drop them from their life.

While the narcissist verges on grandiosity they often suffer from deep shame. They seek attention to offset their shame. When people challenge them, or let them down in any way, it is seen as a threat to their ego. They typically respond in anger, often rage, but they will rarely apologize for their behavior because that would be too humiliating. They rather lose the relationship.

This can be quite confusing if you don't know what's going on inside the narcissist. It's baffling to see the ease in which they can break off a relationship. I personally observed this in an acquaintance of mine. I had never seen such intense anger in a person, lacking any remorse or desire to restore their relationships. This person was even able to

---

[23] R. A. Emmons, *Personality and Forgiveness* in *Forgiveness: Theory, Research and Practice* (Guildford) p. 164

dismiss family members rather than humble himself and admit wrong.

The narcissist lacks humility and empathy: two keys to forgiveness[24]. Because of this, the narcissist often stays stuck in multiple broken relationships. If you are in relationship with a narcissist, chances are you feel stuck. You keep trying to reconcile with them but with no luck, continually frustrated why nothing seems to work. Take caution. You might be in over your head with this person. Seek counsel to consider alternatives.

Write it down:

- *Do any of the narcissistic tendencies look familiar to you: either in yourself or others?*

- *Have you ever had people confront you on some of these tendencies?*

- *If you are involved with a narcissist what is your plan to work with them?*

4. Passive-Aggressive Behavior

In his book, *Kids in Danger*, Dr. Ross Campbell writes about what he calls "The Anger Ladder." He lists fourteen rungs on the Anger Ladder, ranging from the worst behavior on the bottom rung to the best behavior at the top rung.

The idea is, as you climb the ladder, you improve the way you express

---

[24] LeRon Shults and Stephen Sandage, *Faces of Forgiveness* (Baker Academic) p. 58,59

your anger. At the top rung you express your anger by being pleasant, seeking resolution, focusing anger on the source, holding to the primary complaint, and thinking logically. As you go down the ladder, negative actions replace the positive ones.

For example, at the seventh rung a person is unpleasant and loud, displacing anger to other sources, expressing unrelated complaints, and showing emotionally destructive behavior. At the thirteenth rung (second to the bottom) a person is unpleasant and loud, cursing, displacing anger to other sources, destroying property, verbally abusive, and still showing emotionally destructive behavior.

What do you think the behavior is at the 14th and bottom rung? How can things get any worse than destroying property, cursing, and emotionally destructive behavior? In my seminar I ask people that question, and they always guess murder. Murder would definitely be worse! But short of murder, what do you think it is? Campbell says it's *passive-aggressive behavior*.

Dr. Campbell says that passive-aggressive behavior is "the absolute worst way to handle anger." It is the "opposite of open, honest, direct, and verbal expression of anger." Passive aggressive behavior is when you express your anger, but it's not directed at the person you are mad at. You might use sarcastic humor, slam doors, or kick the dog. You are *aggressive* in that you actively express your anger, but you are *passive* because your anger isn't directed at the source of your anger.

How is it that passive-aggressive behavior is worse than destroying property? It's because when I'm throwing plates across the room, I may be destroying property, but at least you know I'm angry! When you know I'm angry, you can address my anger. However, if I'm slamming doors and sarcastic, you have no idea why if I don't tell you. You can't address the problem if you don't know a problem exists. This is why people often get stuck in anger; they never communicate it effectively in the first place.

Dr. Campbell said:
> The best way to express anger is to do it as pleasantly and rationally as possible, and toward the person one is angry at.

You hope that the person receiving the anger will respond in an equally mature way, attempt to understand the other's position, and that the two can resolve the issue. Resolving the issue means for both parties to rationally and logically examine the issue, discuss it, understand it from both points of view, and to come to an agreement on what to do about it.[25]

Does that sound impossible? If so, that's only because it's never been modeled for you, or you've never developed the habit. It's like watching a concert pianist play the piano if you've never played piano before. You look at them and say, "That's impossible." No, it's not. It just takes work. You can do it!

Write it down:

- *Are you passive aggressive with your anger?*

- *If so, how has passive-aggressive behavior affected your relationships? Do you believe it is part of the reason you are stuck in your anger?*

- *What can you do to change your behavior?*

5. Indecision

In the book, *Necessary Endings*, Henry Cloud writes that one reason people stay stuck is they are unable to decide between two incompatible wishes. Because they are unwilling to choose one idea over the other they remain frozen in place, unable to move on. He says:

You have to be able to face losing some things you might want

---

[25] Dr. Ross Campbell, *Kids in Danger*, (Cook Communications)

in order to be free to do the right thing. If you can't, you stay stuck.[26]

This is such a simple principle. The simplest principles are often the most powerful. If you have trouble moving forward maybe it's because you have two ideas in conflict, and you are unwilling to choose one over the other. Here are a few examples of being stuck in indecision:

- You want to forgive because you know it's the right thing to do. But if you forgive, you believe you will be letting your offender off the hook.

- You want to break up with your boyfriend because he abuses you. But if you break up with him then you will have to go back to work, and you are afraid you won't find a job.

- You want to move closer to your family to have a better support system. But whenever you mention moving your friends tell you how foolish that is.

Maybe you can relate to one of these dilemmas. You are paralyzed to move. Choosing one over the other is what might get you unstuck.

Write it down:

- *Are you stuck in life due to your inability to choose?*

- *What steps can you take to help you make a decision?*

6. Vows

Words have a powerful way of setting you free or keeping you stuck. How many people have been burned in a relationship and vowed, "I'll never let myself be vulnerable again"? It's understandable. People want to protect themselves. Vows are surprisingly effective.

---

[26] Dr. Henry Cloud, *Necessary Endings*, (Harris Business) p. 177

Vows are powerful choices that seem to flip a switch in the brain and prevent you from being injured in the same way. I've counseled many people that were stuck emotionally. As we prayed and processed their pain, we traced the blockage to a vow that was made years ago.

Vows come in many shapes and sizes. The other day I finished teaching on the power of forgiveness when someone said to me, "Well, I can't forgive this person." I've heard that so many times. I had to call them on it. I said, "Is that true? You can't?" "Well, no," she said, "I just don't want to." Ahhh…big difference.

Saying, "I can't" is really a vow to not do something. We say, "I can't" to justify in our mind why we won't. It's our subconscious way of resolving an inconsistency in our logic. We know we don't want to forgive (or whatever it is we are facing), but we know it's not a good enough reason. So, we tell ourselves "I can't." That works much better for us, and we hope it convinces others as well. Or we might come up with a false reason like "I can't forgive because it's unforgiveable." Sounds convincing, but is that really true?

Saying, "I won't" is more honest. It reminds us that we are making a choice and forces us to take responsibility for it. We are *choosing* our future. Sometimes we don't want to admit that. Saying, "I can't" implies there is no choice involved. There's nothing we can do about it. It removes any sense of guilt or responsibility. It's much easier to live with ourselves when we think we can't do something, but it's not honest. It's a form of denial.

Be careful what you vow, and be careful what you say. If you remember a vow you've made, bring it to God. Tell him you are taking the vow back. It will free your mind to move on.

Write it down:

- *Have you made any vows of self-protection that might be keeping you stuck?* Often vows are simply thoughts made in a moment of hurt. You typically aren't aware of them being vows at the time. Pray right now, and ask God to remind you of any vows you've made.

- *Do you hear yourself saying, "I can't"? Do you use this phrase as a form of denial?*

- If you've made any vows stop right now and tell God that you want to break the vow and move on with your life.

7. Evil

Depending on your spiritual beliefs you may or may not believe in personal evil. Skip this section if you like, but Jesus believed in evil and so it's important to address it.

Jesus spoke of the reality of personal evil he called Satan. The Bible tells us Satan is actively working against God and anyone who seeks to follow God. I don't understand that. It seems strange and hard to believe at times, but I've seen the impact of Satan in people's lives, especially in regard to anger.

There are two Bible verses that imply Satan (or the devil) uses anger to undermine us spiritually. In the book of Ephesians, Paul tells the church:

> Be angry, but do not sin; do not let the sun go down on your anger, and give no opportunity to the devil. Ephesians 4:26

Paul doesn't say what kind of opportunity anger gives the devil. In the context of his letter, the implication is the devil uses anger to divide people, breaking up the unity of the church community. That's why it's important to deal with anger each day and not let it accumulate.

In another letter, Paul cautioned the church to offer forgiveness in order to not let the devil take advantage of them. Speaking of the devil he said:
> ...we are not ignorant of his designs. 2 Corinthians 2:11

If you read the context, Paul implies the devil's designs have to do with fostering unforgiveness and disunity.

It's important for us to realize Satan can use our personal anger to undermine our relationships as well as the church community. If being relational is at the core of God's nature then it only makes sense that the best way to attack God is by trying to undermine relationships.

I mention evil here to cause you to think about the source of your relational breakdowns. In some instances, more than we know, there is evil working against us. The Bible alerts us to the fact that:
> Our fight is not against people on earth, but against the rulers and authorities and the powers of this world's darkness, against the spiritual powers of evil in the heavenly world. Ephesians 6:12 New Century Version (NCV)

I'm concerned for this generation because it's often ignorant to the dark side of spirituality and therefore vulnerable to it. Many people are now stuck in anger not knowing why it has such a deep root in them. The good news is Jesus overcame these dark powers. Our faith in him enables us to walk away from the pull of evil and its effect on us.

Write it down:
- *Have you ever engaged in an activity that you feel may have invited evil into your life?*

- *Do you sense a negative force working in you or against you?*

- It's beyond the scope of this book to take this topic any further, but you might want to consider two books: *Steps to Freedom in Christ* by Neil Anderson and *Healing Life's Hurts* by Ed Smith.

Tom's Dilemma

I opened this section talking about Tom's dilemma. After initially going out of his way to help his daughter, he decided to not jump at her demands. He laid down boundaries. He also decided to move out of state to help establish a healthier setting for his other children. After he told me his story, he asked me what I thought. I told him I would do exactly the same thing. He loved his daughter and made that clear, but he couldn't let her chaos dissolve his life. He needed to take action to secure his family no matter what other people said. He couldn't let their opinions control his life.

Tom was able to make a tough choice that freed him to move forward. By making that choice, he now has a chaos-free home his daughter can join should she ever want to return. I hope you also will make the tough choices necessary to secure your future.

Part Two

UNSTUCK

The story of Aron Ralston is told in the 2010 movie, *127 Hours*. Aron is the climber who got his arm caught under a boulder while hiking in Utah. After being stuck for 127 hours he freed himself by amputating his own arm with a small knife.

His situation looked impossible. There was no way out. His predicament would have certainly ended in death, but he did the unthinkable and regained his life. After watching the movie you understand why he had to do what he did, but it didn't make it any easier to watch.

My point: getting unstuck isn't always pretty, and it takes a lot of hard work, *but it's possible*.

Chapter Fourteen:

The Foolishness of Forgiveness

After speaking to a small group about forgiveness I was taken aback by the level of *un*-forgiveness I heard in two people. They spoke in no uncertain terms of their desire to see their offenders mercilessly destroyed.

It's interesting to me how I can teach for days about forgiveness, only to realize I'm not making *any* headway with people. They carefully take notes but inside say, *This doesn't apply to me.* Some people have decided...no, it's stronger than that, have VOWED, to not forgive. In their mind you'd be a fool to forgive.

They have no idea what this attitude does to them. When I encounter this kind of resistance it reminds me that forgiveness is *spiritual* and not a simple three-step process.

My class included a sixty-five-year old man and a twenty-year-old girl: both trapped in bitter anger. The man's father had abused him as a child. The girl had been raped. The man hated his father his entire life, and it showed in every deep line on his face. I hoped the girl saw this. I wanted to ask her...*Is this what you want to look like in forty-five years? Is your bitterness and resentment worth the cost of what you will pay over the next five decades?*

Her hatred didn't hurt her offender, only her.

Of course, I understood her reaction. The violation of rape is incomprehensible to me. She had the right to her anger. I just didn't want her to embrace it forever and let it slowly destroy her life. There is a saying: *Unforgiveness is like drinking poison and expecting your offender to die.* I was afraid she was drinking the poison.
This girl was so young and had so much life ahead of her. I have daughters her age. I would hate to have either one of them consumed with the level of hatred I saw in her.

Even if she could retaliate, what would that achieve? She would then have to deal with the guilt and consequences. Plus, she would reduce herself to her offender's level. That's not a win. It's just one more loss added to the tragedy.

Marrying herself to her abuser through hatred and revenge was not the answer. Her anger only invited him back into her life every day to abuse her emotionally one more time. The best thing she could do for herself was to forgive: take back her life, and let God deal with her offender.

But she wasn't able to see this. Forgiving her offender was too much to ask. It made no sense. The idea was actually offensive, like I was in some way excusing her offender. It was as if she was saying, "Don't lay that religious crap on me. Can't you see I'm hurting?" To her, forgiveness was just another burden laid across her back. That was sad for me to see because that's the last thing I wanted for her. I suggested forgiveness to help remove the burden she carried. I wanted nothing more than for her to get her life back.

The Role Of Forgiveness
Undoubtedly, people do use forgiveness as a religious quick-fix to "make nice" of a tragic situation. I agree that approach is simplistic

and offensive. That's not what I'm talking about here. Forgiveness is important to accomplish three things:
1. **Reclaim your life**. Forgiveness helps you separate emotionally from the pain of an offense as well as your offender.
2. **Reconcile with your offender**. Forgiveness clears the way for the *possibility* of reuniting with your offender.
3. **Rehabilitate your offender**. Forgiveness can *potentially* free your offender to live a new life if they choose to do so.

In many cases, only the first goal is ever achieved, but that alone is significant, even life-changing. If reconciliation and/or rehabilitation are achieved then that should be celebrated even more.

Moving on...

Up until now, I've helped you see what gets you stuck. In the rest of the book we'll work to get you *unstuck*.

Forgiveness: What it is

It was a perfect sunny day in Wisconsin; at least as "perfect" a day can be when it's five degrees below zero. Freezing temperatures mean little when it's your first day skiing.

My daughter's class took a day to visit a local ski hill. She was excited. Always one for adventure, Becca couldn't wait to hit the slopes. My wife and I were happy for her and confident her school leaders and chaperones could help her navigate the ropes of this new sport.

Becca was expertly equipped in the rental shop and taught on the basics with a lesson on the bunny slope. Then it was time for her solo descent. She did so well her friend said she should go down the intermediate hill. A bit hesitant, she agreed, but something went terribly wrong on the way down.

When the ski area first called me they said there had been an accident. I thought, *Okay, kids break their arms or legs. That's not the worst thing.*

She will survive. Then they said they were flying in a helicopter from the Trauma Center in St. Paul because there could be brain trauma. They would call us when the helicopter picked her up.

Becca hit a tree. She lost control and went flying into the woods. Her head and hands took the full impact. We found out later that she cracked her skull, broke her nose, cracked her eye socket, broke her fingers and wrist, and bruised her brain (worse than a concussion). Suddenly I wasn't so confident that neither she nor I would survive this event. I called my wife with the news. We met at our house and waited for the call.

Forty-five minutes later the phone rang. The ski patrol told us the helicopter was busy, so they took Becca to Luther Hospital in Eau Claire, a medium-size town halfway between our house and the ski area. That actually upset me. I didn't like the fact she had to go to the Trauma Center, but if she needed that level of care then that's where I wanted her to go.

My wife and I went to the Emergency Room where we had to wait while they treated Becca. When they wheeled her to another room we caught a glimpse of her. She looked like she had been beaten up; her face was swollen and purple. I still tear up every time I tell the story. I have so many emotions tied to the memory; I can't help myself.

That night many people from school came to see Becca. She attended a church school where I was on the pastoral staff. It made things awkward because many of the people with her that day were members at my church.

Despite being their pastor I found myself getting madder and madder as each person entered Becca's room to express their condolences. I'll be honest; I wasn't exactly full of mercy and grace that night. I was angry. I know accidents happen, but I kept wondering how the chaperones and ski instructors could let a novice skier go down an intermediate hill. I kept asking myself, *What were they thinking? Where were they? How could they let this happen? I trusted them to watch out for my girl, and they let me down.*

Hitting a tree is serious. Thirty-seven skiers died that winter for that reason. Thankfully, Becca recovered. The "only" long-term impact was she lost her sense of smell due to the olfactory nerve being severed between her nose and brain.

When Life Throws You A Curveball

If you are a parent my guess is you can feel the terror of this story. Maybe you've been in a situation like this where you were unable to protect or defend your child. It's the worst feeling: *gut wrenching*. It took me a while to forgive the people in charge that day.

As I have reflected on what incidents are the hardest to forgive, I concluded it has to be anything that impacts my children in a negative way. I can handle people who hurt me. It's a different story when it comes to my kids.

The reason I tell you this story is to alert you to the fact that you never know when life will throw you a curve, and anger will take you prisoner. When it does, you quickly learn that forgiveness doesn't come easily.

Forgiveness is Great...for the Other Guy

Forgiveness is something people talk about, but I don't know how much we actually do it. It's a great concept for *other* people, but when *we* are the person hurt we often find a reason why forgiveness doesn't apply to us. C.S. Lewis said:
> Everyone says forgiveness is a lovely idea, until they have something to forgive.[27]

People often say something like, *I know I should forgive, BUT...* and then a variety of answers finish the sentence:
> *It hurts too much.*
> *The other person isn't sorry for what they did.*
> *If I forgive them they'll just do it again.*
> *What they did was unforgiveable.*

Forgiveness is something to offer, not just talk about. We can't be

---

[27] C. S. Lewis, *Mere Christianity*, (HarperOne), Book 3, Chapter 7

people who celebrate God's forgiveness on Sunday and hold a grudge on Monday. That's so self-serving: using God's forgiveness for our own benefit but refusing to share it with others. No, we *celebrate* God's forgiveness by *offering* it to others. If we have any hope of getting unstuck, it will involve either forgiving or *being* forgiven. One way or the other, forgiveness will be a part of the story.

Defining Forgiveness

Many people never forgive because they misunderstand forgiveness. They have too many layers of false information and assumptions that make forgiveness sound too complicated, even impossible. I want to help you cut through these layers by giving you a clear definition of what forgiveness is.

It's hard to reduce forgiveness to one simple definition, so I offer you four.

1. Forgiveness means removing the offense.

Let's start by looking at something Jesus said:

> ...when you stand praying, if you **hold anything against anyone**, forgive him, so that your Father in heaven may forgive you your sins. Mark 11:25 (emphasis added)

According to Jesus, forgiveness is the *opposite* of holding something against someone. It means to let go of the event or events that separate you from another person. Think of literally holding up a big sign with your offender's faults written all over it. This sign defines your relationship with them. Whenever you encounter them, you are quick to point to the sign reminding them of what they did and how things are no longer the same between the two of you. You won't let them forget. They owe you, and you hold them accountable.

Jesus tells us it is our responsibility to remove this sign that stands between us. If we don't, we not only block our relationship with the other person, we block our relationship with God as well: a sobering thought.

2. Forgiveness means giving up the right to get even.

When you are offended you naturally want justice. You want to balance the scales. You look for payback. You don't want your offender to get away with something, and so you take it upon yourself to exact judgment. Who else can do this job as well as you?

But forgiveness says, *No, I'm not going to get even. I'm not going to retaliate or teach them a lesson. I'm not going to seek an "eye for an eye." I'm going to release my offender from any sense of payback, if indeed they can pay me back. I'm going to trust God will make up for my loss and deal with them in his own way, in his own time.*

Now, you might say you never try to get even when people offend you. That's admirable, but let me challenge you. Do any of these sound familiar?

- The silent treatment.
- Avoiding your offender.
- Speaking badly about them.
- Exposing their weaknesses.
- Destroying their reputation.
- Withholding love or kindness from them.
- Sabotaging their success.
- Terminating the relationship.
- Turning children against them.
- Speaking to them in a patronizing or sarcastic way.
- Excluding them.
- Putting them on a guilt trip.
- Withholding necessary information.
- Making them jump through hoops.

These are just a few subtle ways we use to get even. You might want to reread the list again because the first time through you were probably in denial! Read it, and be honest. Think about your offender. Do you find yourself doing any of these things? (Circle the ones you do.)

3. Forgiveness means giving up the right to have your offender solve your problems.

Some people spend their entire lives insisting their mom, dad, ex-wife, boss, etc. fully apologize for what they did and make everything right. It's not realistic. It probably won't happen. The problem with this expectation is you spend your life waiting for someone else to make you happy. You've handed over control of your emotional state to another person. Your own inability to forgive locks you in a prison of your own making. How smart is that?

But forgiveness enables you to separate from your offender and move on in life. Beverly Flanigan says:
> What does the choice to forgive really mean? It means you no longer expect the person who injured you owes you anything. It means you don't look back. You no longer look at why the injury happened; you now look at what you will do and who you will be in the future.[28]

Then she says:
> Forgiveness is a closure. It closes a door and releases you to start fresh.[29]

Jesus taught us to pray, *forgive us our debts as we forgive our debtors* (Matthew 6:12). He tells us that forgiveness cancels a debt. It eliminates it, takes it off the books, like an accountant erasing a payment due. We don't forget about it. We refuse to focus on it and insist on repayment.

If you've ever held out for your friend to pay you back $50, you know what I mean. You hint. You ask politely. They promise "tomorrow," but it never happens. You can continue to press the issue, but is it really worth it? You are wise to cancel the debt and move on with your life. Your time and mental energy is worth much more than $50. The same is true in dealing with offenses.

4. Forgiveness means letting go of the past and moving into the future.

Desmond Tutu has a book entitled *No Future without Forgiveness*. The

---

[28] *Forgiving the Unforgivable*, p. 144
[29] Ibid. p. 148

title alone speaks volumes. When there is no forgiveness, you are trapped in your past. You are held hostage in a web of bitterness, resentment, and hatred. The strange thing is you are your own kidnapper. Your friends and family sit by unable to help you because there is no ransom they can pay. You are preoccupied with what *was* instead of what *might be*, and it keeps you stuck in the past.

It's like driving a car down the road with an oversized rearview mirror blocking your view of the road. All you see is where you were, not where you are headed. If you allow that to happen, you are headed for a certain crash.

You can prevent this crash. It doesn't have to happen. By forgiving your offender you will regain the proper perspective and move freely into your future.

Two Words

There are two Greek words in the Bible that are translated "forgive." Looking at them might help us with our definition.

The first word is *apheimi*: which means to **send away**,
> ...forgive (*apheimi*) us our debts, as we also have forgiven (*apheimi*) our debtors. Matthew 6:12

It's easy for an offense to become so big in your mind that it's all you think about when you see or think about your offender. It's as if their offense is written across their forehead. The offense and the offender are inseparable in your mind. We need to "send away" the offense: to detach the offense from their identity.

The truth is your offender is much more than their offense. It's not fair to define them by that one offense. How would you like it if people reduced you to the single worst act you've ever done in your life? Is that how you want to be defined? Of course not. That would be devastating, yet we do that to other people all the time. It's not fair. We want people to "send away" our offenses and we should do the same for them.

To refuse to send your offender's offense away is like cursing them. You label them with their sin for life. When people sense your unwillingness to forgive, they often choose to not change. It's like the teenager who says, "My parents don't think I'll ever change, so why bother trying?" When you forgive your offender, you separate them from their offense. Forgiveness frees the offender to become a better person.

The second word is *apoluo*: which means to **divorce** or **release**.
> Forgive (*apoluo*) and you will be forgiven (*apoluo*). Luke 6:37

An offense has an interesting effect on you. In one sense, it separates you from your offender. In another sense, it *binds* you closer to them, wedding you to them emotionally. As much as you want to distance yourself from them, the memory of what they did haunts you even years after the event. It's as if you've lined your house with pictures of your offender, only the pictures are in your mind. You've become frozen in the moment of the offense; you are stuck.

Forgiveness enables you to separate from your offender: freeing you to move on in life. It divorces you from an unhealthy bond: an unholy alliance.

Forgiveness is a simple concept, but it can be complex because it often happens in layers rather than all at once. It's a process where you need to patiently work your way through the layers over time. But it's worth the effort.

Write it down:
- *As you read through the definitions of forgiveness, which ones stand out to you the most? Why?*

- *Who are the people in your life you've reduced to a single label because of what they did to you?* Write them down.

- Ask God to help you send the offenses away from each person.

- List the people that you have become wedded to through unforgiveness.

- Ask God to break the spiritual/emotional ties to them.

Forgiveness: What it is not

Susan came to me after hearing me teach on forgiveness. She said, "I know I need to forgive, but I can't." Her husband had abused drugs, lost thousands of dollars, and put their family in great jeopardy. Whenever he did drugs, he became a threat to her family, and she couldn't let him back in her life.

Susan was a kind person. She loved her husband and children. She didn't wish her husband harm. She just didn't want to allow him to destroy her life or the life of her kids. Susan was making the mistake that many people make: she couldn't forgive her husband because she misunderstood forgiveness. Before I tell you what happened to Susan let me explain what forgiveness is not.

1. Forgiveness is Not Forgetting

Some people think all you have to do to forgive is just forget what happened. Maybe someone has said that to you… *Just forget about it. What's the problem? Why can't you get over it!* They might even quote the Bible where God said:

> For I will forgive their wickedness and will remember their sins no more. Jeremiah 31:34.

These people say you just need to do what God does…*forget*. But when offended people hear this, they often shut down. They say, *If forgiveness is contingent on my forgetting, then I can never forgive because I'll never forget what was done to me.*

Look back at the verse from Jeremiah. It doesn't say God *forgets* our sin. It says he *chooses to not remember it*. There's a big difference between that and forgetting.

When it comes to the big hurts in life, we don't forgive and forget.

We forgive what we *can't* forget.

We can forget the little offenses. It's the big offenses that stick with us. The big offenses need something more powerful than forgetting. They need forgiveness.

2. Forgiveness is Not Excusing

I've seen many people recoil at the thought of forgiveness. They think it sends the message to their offender that what they did wasn't really so bad. This is especially true for victims of abuse and betrayal, but that's not what forgiveness is about.

Let's look at God's forgiveness. God doesn't excuse us. He doesn't minimize what we've done. The Bible gives us many examples of this. In fact, God doesn't hold back in accusing us. Listen to what the apostle Peter said to a group of people speaking about Jesus:

> **You handed him over** to be killed, and **you disowned him** before Pilate, though he had decided to let him go. **You disowned** the Holy and Righteous One and asked that a murderer be released to you. **You killed the author of life**, but God raised him from the dead. Acts 3:13-15 (emphasis added)

Peter's accusation couldn't be any stronger than this. He lays the full blame at the feet of the people who offered up Jesus to death. Yet he still offers forgiveness.

> Now, brothers and sisters, I know that you acted in ignorance, as did your leaders...Repent, then, and turn to God, so that your sins may be wiped out, that times of refreshing may come from the Lord... Acts 3:17-19

God's forgiveness doesn't excuse what we did. God calls it like it is. Miroslav Volf says:

> To forgive is to name and condemn the misdeed...God doesn't just condemn and then forgive. God also condemns in the very

act of forgiving.[30]

Since God's forgiveness doesn't excuse sin, our forgiveness shouldn't either. In the book, *To Forgive is Human*, the authors put it this way:
> Forgiveness acknowledges that moral violations in relationships are wrong. But forgiveness cancels a debt that a person legitimately owes rather than simply lets the person off the hook. Forgiveness does not wink at the moral violation (condoning) or deny the offender's responsibility (exoneration). Forgiveness chooses to cancel a debt that is serious and real.[31]

Both quotes show that forgiveness contains within it an accusation of wrong, not the excuse of wrong that many fear.

If you are afraid your forgiveness will communicate the wrong thing to your offender then be clear with them just like the Bible is clear with us. Outline the severity of what they did, but let them know that you won't hold it against them. You won't treat them like they are less of a person or with any less dignity.

3. Forgiveness is Not Trusting

This might be one of the biggest misunderstandings about forgiveness. I can forgive you immediately, but it takes time to rebuild trust. Put another way; forgiveness is free… trust is earned.

Trust and forgiveness are mutually exclusive, meaning they are not connected or dependent upon each other. You can have one without the other. Just because I forgive you does not necessitate I trust you.

Alcoholics often miss this point. Let's say parents forgive their daughter for her drunken and reckless lifestyle, but when she comes home for a visit they lock the liquor cabinet. When the daughter sees this she is irate. She says, *You said you forgave me, but you lock the liquor cabinet. What hypocrites!*

---

[30] Miroslav Volf, *Free of Charge*, (Zondervan), p. 166
[31] Steven J. Sandage and Everett L. Worthington Jr., *To Forgive is Human*, (IVP Books), p.33

No. The parents aren't hypocrites. The parents understand the difference between forgiveness and trust even though the daughter doesn't.

4. Forgiveness is Not Reunion

Just because I can forgive you doesn't mean we will automatically get back together as friends, business partners, or marriage partners. I might forgive you but determine you have betrayed my trust so much I can't be with you.

I've seen this when one person has an affair outside of marriage. Let's say it's the wife who had the affair and the husband is gracious enough to forgive her. The wife might assume they can just pick up where they left off, but the husband wisely says:

> *I do forgive you...but I can't live with you right now. It's not just the affair; it's the five years of lying and deception surrounding the affair. I need some time apart to allow you to rebuild my trust.*

Sometimes you can forgive someone and be immediately restored. That is certainly the ideal, but sometimes the role of forgiveness is to enable you to move on from an unhealthy person. One author summed up reunion like this:

> It takes one person to forgive...It takes two to be united.
> Forgiving happens inside the wounded person...
> Reunion happens in a relationship between two people.
> We can forgive a person who never says he is sorry...
> We cannot be truly reunited unless he is honestly sorry.
> We can forgive even if we do not trust the person who wronged us once not to wrong us again...
> Reunion can happen only if we can trust the person who wronged us once not to wrong us again.
> Forgiving has no strings attached...Reunion has several strings attached.[32]

5. Forgiveness is Not Conditional

---

[32] Lewis Smedes, *The Art of Forgiving*, (Ballantine Books), p. 47

Forgiveness is not based on what the other person does or doesn't do. Sometimes people tell me they would consider forgiveness if they could get an apology, but *The guy isn't even sorry for what he did.* They might point out verses that connect forgiveness with repentance. For example, Jesus said:
> If your brother sins, rebuke him, and if he repents, forgive him. Luke 17:3

There are other verses like this connecting forgiveness with repentance, but we have to look at the entirety of scripture. I know some people teach you don't have to forgive unless your offender repents. In my opinion that's wrong for two reasons. First, unconditional forgiveness is God's model for us. I mentioned two Greek words for forgiveness before. Here is a third; *charizoma*i, which means "grace" or "gift." Paul used it in his letter to the Ephesian church:
> Be kind and compassionate to one another, forgiving (*charizoma*) each other, just as in Christ God forgave (*charizoma*) you. Ephesians 4:32

This word tells us that your offender can't earn forgiveness. It's not dependent on what they do. It is a gift. Jesus said:
> Freely you have received, freely give. Matthew 10:8

In other words, Jesus didn't ask us to do anything to earn his forgiveness. Why do we insist on others earning our forgiveness? We do this because we are under the false assumption that forgiveness is earned. Be careful, if you think that about others, you will probably think that about you and God too. Trying to earn your forgiveness can make for a very depressing life.

The apostle Paul made it clear to us that God's love is unconditional.
> God demonstrates his own love for us in this: **While we were still sinners**, Christ died for us. Romans 5:8 (emphasis added)

God didn't wait for us to clean up our act before he sent Jesus into the world. He took the first step. Paul communicates the same idea when he says:
> ...it is by grace (*charis*, the root for *charizoma*) you have been saved, through faith--and this is not from yourselves, it is the

- I don't know how to forgive.
- Anger works for me. It gives me the control I want.
- I fear how the relationship may change if I forgive.
- Forgiveness is not my issue.
- My offender never asked to be forgiven.
- They aren't sorry enough.
- I don't want to give them the power in the relationship.
- I don't want to dig up the past.
- I'm afraid of talking to my offender.
- My friends and family tell me not to forgive.
- Forgiveness will make me vulnerable.
- What if they reject me?
- I tried forgiveness before and it didn't work.
- The offense is unforgivable.

I mention all these excuses to warn you your brain has no problem thinking of an excuse. If you don't want to forgive, you can always find a reason not to do it.

Write it down:

- *Of the five myths, which ones do you believe?*

- *What do you think you need to do now you know they are myths?*

- *What are some of the reasons you've chosen not to forgive? Circle the ones above you can relate to.*

Remember Susan? Coincidentally, the day after we met, I just happened to speak on "The Five Things Forgiveness is Not," in church. This is what she wrote me later that week after hearing what I had to say about forgiveness.

> *I am so compelled to write to you today. I am so amazed by how prayers are answered. I have been asking God to bring someone or something into my life to show me signs or give me direction. I was stuck in the mud; I had only healed to a certain point and leveled off. It wasn't enough, so I prayed for more direction.*

gift of God-- not by works, so that no one can b[e]
2:8,9

There is nothing we can do that merits the love or forgi[veness]
That's true for your offender too.

The second reason our forgiveness should be uncondi[tional]
logic. If forgiveness is conditional, it means my offende[r]
As long as my offender doesn't apologize and ask for for[giveness]
chained to him or her emotionally. Let's take this to the [extreme]
say my offender is sinister and wants to mess with my e[motions]
so they say...*If I don't apologize then Remy will stay angry*
resentful and bitter. Remy will think about me the rest of h[is life]
ha.

But forgiveness changes the scenario. Forgiveness sets [me free from]
my offender. Forgiveness gives me the "trump" card. L[ewis Smedes]
helps us here again by saying:

> To forgive is to set a prisoner free and disco[ver the]
> prisoner was you.[33]

This is especially important if you are a victim of abuse or [trauma. The]
temptation is to live in the past, obsessing about what was [done,]
but what you need more than ever is to win back your life
by forgiving, not reenacting the abuse in your mind.

De-Mything Forgiveness

The five statements above are myths that will keep you stu[ck.]
They will give you the excuse you want to harbor resentme[nt. But they]
aren't the only myths. Here are a few more that people [have shared]
with me over the years:

- It hurts too much to forgive.
- I feel like I'd be betraying a friend or family membe[r.]
- It's too risky. I'll lose more than I gain if I forgive.
- I'm not capable of forgiving.
- If I forgive I'll lose my excuses to do what I want to [do.]

---

[33] *Forgive and Forget*, p. 133

I was not in church last Sunday, so I listened to your message last night about forgiveness. Every word of this hit home with me on such a deep level. Your definition of what forgiveness is but more so, the definition of what it is NOT, was so meaningful. In fact, I had such a feeling of peace. I understand now what forgiveness is and how it relates to God, and that was such a missing link for me.

I was dealing with some things in my head today as it relates to the divorce and all the things lost that have made me so angry. I realized today that I really wasn't angry anymore. I had thought before that in order for me to let go of that anger, I had to trust him or excuse it somehow. In hindsight now, that seems foolish, but it was what was happening. I don't trust, but I can choose not to remember like God wrote in the Old Testament. I can allow my ex to build trust. I can let go of the anger and feel peace. It's over. It's all in the past. And if I want to move forward and excel in life, this anger has got to go. So I let it go and God has helped me do it. My shoulders feel relaxed! ha-ha.

I know it will be a continuous process and through prayer I am achieving the strength I need. My ex was here tonight to pick up the kids and I told him about this. I told him that I forgive him. It was a powerful moment.

I am eager to move on with my life and again expect it to be a process, but I made a huge leap out of the mud I was stuck in. I wanted you to know that. Thank you. You are making a huge difference in my life in a short period of time. It's so fantastic to feel fantastic! The grace of God has left me at a loss for words.

You might be like Susan. You might be able to forgive better than you realize once you strip forgiveness of everything it's not.

Chapter Fifteen:

How to Forgive

One of the questions I often get asked is, "How do I forgive?" People know they *should* forgive. What they lack are the practical steps on *how* to forgive.

It's interesting to note that, even though the Bible often commands us to forgive, it never once gives instructions on how to do it. I wonder if the disciples ever stopped Jesus after one of his teachings and said, *Whoa, whoa, whoa...wait a minute. We get that we are supposed to forgive, but what does it actually look like? Are there steps? Is there a process? Give us a little help here!*

That's what I want to give you now, practical steps to forgive. I hesitate to call them "steps" because forgiveness isn't a formula. It's more of an art. Lewis Smedes says:

> Forgiving, when you come down to it, is an art, a practical art, maybe the most neglected of all the healing arts. It is the art of healing inner wounds inflicted by other people's wrongs.[34]

Since forgiveness is an art, let's just call these "suggestions" or "ideas"

---

[34] *The Art of Forgiving*, p.xiii

on how to forgive.

Be The Hero

When you decide to get unstuck you choose to be the hero of your story. It doesn't take any courage to be angry. It doesn't take any skill to complain, gossip, cast blame, or feel sorry for yourself. Anyone can do that.

But is that the story you want your life to tell?

Would you watch a movie for two hours about a person who suffered an injustice, then complained and felt sorry for herself the rest of the movie? Of course not! What makes a good story is when someone faces injustice with wisdom, courage, and grace. We call these people heroes.

So why not be the hero of your own story?

Being the hero requires a choice: *a heroic* choice. It means stepping up and saying, *I'm not going to let my past control me anymore. My anger doesn't help my offender, God, or me. I'm going to forgive and move on with my life.*

Heroic choices free you from being stuck and open your life up to all kinds of possibilities. They make your story compelling. Engaging.

I like what John Trent says about the power good choices have on your life:

> Healthy stories challenge us to be active characters, not passive victims or observers. Both the present and the future are determined by choices, and choice is the essence of character. If we see ourselves as active characters in our own stories, we can exercise our human freedom to choose a present and future for ourselves and for those we love that give life meaning.[35]

---

[35] *Choosing to Live the Blessing*, p. 36

Trent makes the case we should be proactive in choosing our future and not let our future simply happen to us. He builds on this idea of choice when he says:

> We can curse the past like victims of circumstance, or we can bless it like victors over our circumstances. It's up to us. It's our choice. In some of the strongest and most compelling stories, the main character makes life-and-death choices. These choices give the story energy. They make the plot intriguing. They also change the character. The character who doesn't make choices is weak and passive. So if we want our lives to tell strong and compelling stories in which the characters grow into people of blessing, then we – the characters – have to make choices. Choices that are sometimes difficult. Choices that are sometimes painful. Choices that are sometimes critical, where something important is at stake. [36]

If you think of the movies that touch you, they most often reach a moment of decision for the protagonist. In the beginning of the story she struggles with a problem, but there is a "make or break" moment. Against all odds she decides to take a risk and do the right thing. The risk adds tension to the story because it adds a level of doubt. Can she do it? Will she regret her choice?

In the end her choice pays off. You breathe a sigh of relief. Her choice enables her to overcome her struggle and become the hero. That's a story you are willing to pay money to see.

Everyone's life tells a story. You have more control over it than you may think. The choices you make today determine who you will be in the future. The question is: are you making choices that tell a good story?

Here are three choices that are central to becoming the hero of your story.

---

[36] Ibid. p. 66

1. Choose to Admit Your Anger

Admitting your anger isn't as easy as it sounds. No one likes to admit they are angry. It's embarrassing, like you lack self-control. Plus, once you admit your anger, people expect you to work on it. We don't always like that kind of pressure. It's easier to live in denial, but admitting is always the first step to change so:

> *Quit ignoring it: hoping it will disappear.*
> *Quit minimizing it: acting like it's not a big deal.*
> *Quit rationalizing it: thinking you can explain it away.*
> *Quit medicating it: hoping you can numb the pain.*
> *Quit blaming others: expecting others to take care of it for you.*

As long as you refuse to admit your anger, it will lay in the weeds and surface when you least expect it. It reminds me of what I read about the fields in Cambodia. During the Vietnam War hundreds of thousands of landmines were laid in the Cambodian fields. Still today, thousands lie unexploded, waiting for some unwary person (mostly children) to happen upon them. As a result, countless children have lost their legs and arms and even died due to these mines.

In the same way, your anger lies quietly waiting for the right circumstances to explode and do damage in your life. What you thought was long gone is painfully present. The only way to keep people safe in Cambodia is to dig up the landmines. The same is true for your anger. If you want to be a hero, admit your anger and deal with it.

Write it down:

- *What's preventing you from admitting your anger? What's the fear?*

- *What are the excuses you use to keep from dealing with your anger?*

- *Have you seen your anger recur after you thought you had dealt with it?*

2. Choose to Own Your Loss

To "own your loss" means to take responsibility for it. Heroes choose to quit blaming people and playing the victim. Heroes work on a solution.

Owning the loss is a hard step to take because it's easy to say:
> Hey, this isn't my problem. This is their problem. They hurt me. I didn't hurt them. I'm going to sit right here and make them come back and fix what they broke.

You can do that, and in some cases it might work, but what if they don't fix what's broken? How long are you going to sit there and wait? How long are you going to let other people control your life, holding you hostage?

Imagine that I loan you my car. Then you crash it and leave it in some parking lot. You drop the keys off at my house and casually tell me what happened but make no offer to repair the car. I sit in my house and have a big pity party. I tell everyone how unfair you are. I call my boss and tell him I can't come to work because you wrecked my car. I run out of groceries and go hungry because I can't make it to the market. My life quickly goes downhill because I don't have a car to get around.

The problem started because of what you did, but who is to blame now? It's me. Sure, you should have done something, and it's right of me to expect and ask that of you, but once I see you have no intention of helping me then I need to take responsibility. I have to quit playing the victim and own the loss.

Don't let what other people do to you be an excuse to be lazy, passive, or even worse: self-destructive. It's hard to forgive when you are stuck and you know it's your offender's responsibility. But once you take responsibility, and move on with your life, you'll find it's easier to forgive. It's freeing to take back control of your life. That's what heroes do.

Write it down:
- *What losses have you failed to own? How has failure to own these losses affected your life?*

- *What can you do to start owning these losses?*

3. Choose to Accept God's Help

Heroes aren't afraid to accept help. Heroes know what they face is bigger than they are and will accept all the help they can get...especially from God.

It took me a number of years to understand that God is personal and wants to be involved in my life. In some ways it makes no sense. Why would God care about someone as insignificant as me? But that's what the Bible says: God cares deeply.

There are many reasons why people never accept God's help:
- ***They don't know how to ask for help.*** People think there must be some complicated ritual or formula to making contact with God.
- ***They don't know how to connect to something invisible.*** They consider themselves scientifically minded. If they can't touch or test something then it's not real to them.
- ***They feel unworthy of connecting with God.*** They assume God is unhappy with them and wants nothing to do with them.
- ***They are afraid they won't be able do what they want to do.*** They fear turning into a religious robot that mindlessly parrots some church leader and obeys a list of meaningless rules.
- ***They assume that God doesn't care.*** If God allows bad things to happen then why should they turn to him now? He obviously doesn't care or has no power to effect change.

In spite of all the reasons not to include God in your life, what have you got to lose? This might be just the opportunity God will use to reveal himself to you. Why not ask God to help you get unstuck and be the hero of your story? Ask him to show himself to you in ways you can see him and understand him. Then pay attention! If you are sincere and give God a chance (weeks and months, not hours) you'll see God show up in your life.

Write it down:
- *What makes it hard for you to turn to God with your anger?*

- *When you think about turning to God for help; do you know how? Here's a simple prayer you can pray to invite God into your situation:*

Father, I'm really mad. I'm hurt, and I don't know what to do. I've got some bad thoughts - some hateful and hurtful thoughts. Please forgive me for them. Father, I didn't ask for the mess I'm in, but it's mine now, and so I choose to take responsibility for my life. I'm not going to let someone else control my destiny. With Your help, I'm taking back my life today. Give me wisdom and strength to make good choices. Amen

Two Beliefs...*to help you be the hero*

It's been said: *what you believe about God determines the person you will become.* If you want to become the hero of your story then here are two beliefs about God that will help.

1. God Is In Control

If God is in control then, no matter what happens, you will eventually come out on top: even if that means you die and join God in heaven. If you are convinced you can't be defeated then you are free to forgive. No person or event can ruin you or define you. There is no need for you to pay them back in any way. You can get on with your life trusting that God will work things out. There's no benefit in you spending any time obsessing about your loss.

The Bible backs up this idea when it says:
> God causes everything to work together for the good of those who love God and are called according to his purpose for them. Romans 8:28 New Living Translation (NLT)

No matter what happens in your life, God is the ultimate Restorer. He has an amazing way of taking broken pieces and fitting them into a beautiful mosaic. If you believe this, no one can defeat you. The Bible puts it like this:
> If God is for us, who can be against us? He who did not spare his own Son, but gave him up for us all--how will he not also, along with him, graciously give us all things? Who will bring any charge against those whom God has chosen? It is God who justifies. Who then can condemn? No one. Romans 8:31-33

God will stop at nothing to help us, even coming in the form of a human (Jesus). The Bible continues:
> Who shall separate us from the love of Christ? Shall trouble or hardship or persecution or famine or nakedness or danger or sword? ...No, in all these things we are more than conquerors through him who loved us. Romans 8:35,37

Notice that these verses make no promise to eliminate hardship from our lives. The implication is: hardship doesn't mean God has lost control. It is "in all these things" that we are more than conquerors. We conquer by *overcoming* our obstacles, not avoiding them. So setbacks don't automatically mean we are headed for a fall because God always has our back. God assures us:
> Don't be afraid, for I am with you. Do not be dismayed, for I am your God. I will strengthen you. I will help you. I will uphold you with my victorious right hand. Isaiah 41:10

Now you might object; *If God is in control then why did he let my loss happen in the first place?* In fact, a big part of your anger might be at God for letting the loss occur. People ask me all the time, *How could God let this happen? Why didn't he intervene?*

I answer this with an analogy of giving birth to a child and the doctor giving you two options. The doctor says:

> *We have a new technology you might be interested in. We can implant a chip in your child that will make him conform to all your wishes. He will always obey you. He will never get in trouble and will succeed at everything he does. For an extra fee we can even preprogram sentences of love and admiration he will communicate to you on demand.*

There's a tremendous upside to this offer. This chip would eradicate 99% of all parental problems. Would you choose this option? I've related this analogy to many people, and no one has liked this option. Why not? Because it eliminates free will. Your child would be a robot following a program. People tell me they would forego the chip and risk rebellion, crime, and even the death of their child rather than eliminate free will.

Though inadequate to fully address the pain of "Where was God?" I hope this analogy helps explain how God can be in control even when bad things happen. God could intervene and occasionally does (i.e. miracles), but to preserve our free will he allows natural consequences to play-out from our choices. Rather than prevent tragedy from happening, God works with us on the backside of tragedy to help us through it. Then one Day he will return to set everything right.

2. God Forgives You

The second belief about God that will help you to forgive is knowing God forgives *you*. One of the reasons people have trouble forgiving others is they haven't received God's forgiveness for themselves. It's hard to give away what you don't have. On the other hand, if you are aware of your own ability to fail and have experienced God's forgiveness, then you are more inclined to pass on the gift you've enjoyed yourself.

Many people struggle believing God forgives them. I want to share some of my favorite Bible passages with you about forgiveness. God says:

> I, even I, am he who blots out your transgressions, for my own

> sake, and remembers your sins no more. Isaiah 43:25
>
> Pay attention... I, the LORD, made you, and I will not forget to help you. I have swept away your sins like the morning mists. I have scattered your offenses like the clouds. Oh, return to me, for I have paid the price to set you free. Isaiah 44:21,22 NLT
>
> I will cleanse them from all the sin they have committed against me and will forgive all their sins ... Jeremiah 33:8
>
> As far as the east is from the west, so far has God removed our sins from us. Psalm 103:12
>
> "Come now, let us reason together," says the LORD. "Though your sins are like scarlet, they shall be as white as snow; though they are red as crimson, they shall be like wool. Isaiah 1:18
>
> If we confess our sins, he is faithful and just and will forgive us our sins and purify us from all unrighteousness. 1 John 1:9.

If you struggle believing you are forgiven, I hope you will commit these verses to memory.

Here's an analogy that might put God's forgiveness in perspective. Imagine a bar graph recording everything you've ever done wrong. Put a number on it. Let's say it contains 300,000 terrible things!

Now, on another graph, put a bar that measures God's forgiveness. Where would you cap the bar on God's forgiveness? You can't cap it. Why? Because God is infinite. There's no end to his forgiveness. You can't put a limit on it.

You, on the other hand, are finite. Your sin has a limit. No matter how much you sin, the moment you die your sin will come to an end.
So here's the good news; God's forgiveness will always be greater than your sin. God's forgiveness always trumps your sin. You can't out-sin God's forgiveness. You can try, but you can't do it.

You might object. You might say you don't deserve to be forgiven. Of course you don't! No one deserves to be forgiven! Forgiveness is a gift. You can't earn it. You just receive it. Once you truly understand what God has done in forgiving you – once your heart has been softened by his love – it will be much easier to pass that same love onto someone else who doesn't deserve to be forgiven either.

Think back to when you were a child at Christmas. Remember opening presents. Did you ever stop and say, *Oh, I don't deserve this present. I can't accept it?* Most likely not. You ripped open the package and carted the gift off to your room. Do the same thing with God's forgiveness. Don't hesitate to accept it. Don't question your worthiness. Just accept God's forgiveness, thank him for it, and don't ever talk yourself out of it.

If you struggle with feeling forgiven then let's address that right now with a prayer:

> *Father, You know all about my shortcomings. I haven't been able to shake the guilt of my past, but I'm trusting Your forgiveness will provide me with the relief I need. Your word says Your forgiveness is free of charge, so I'm going to take you up on the offer. Thank You for Your kindness to me. Help me to believe it in the depths of my heart and then offer this same forgiveness to others.*

Asking for forgiveness sets you free. Choosing to forgive others makes you a hero.

Joseph Was A Hero

One of the most famous heroes in the Bible is Joseph. His story was popularized in the Broadway show *Joseph and the Technicolor Dreamcoat.* Put simply, Joseph was abandoned by his brothers and left for dead. He was rescued and ended up in Egypt. Through a series of events he became second in command of the entire nation. During a famine, his brothers traveled to Egypt to find food and ended up encountering Joseph. He could have easily retaliated out of spite and bitterness. Instead, Joseph made a heroic choice to forgive.

> His brothers then came and threw themselves down before him. "We are your slaves," they said. But Joseph said to them,

> "Don't be afraid. Am I in the place of God? You intended to harm me, but God intended it for good to accomplish what is now being done, the saving of many lives. So then, don't be afraid. I will provide for you and your children." And he reassured them and spoke kindly to them. Genesis 50:18-21

Joseph made the heroic choice to accept his situation in life, see God's hand in it, and forgive his brothers. Is that something you could do?

Beverly Flanigan sums up this idea of being a hero when she says:
> Forgiving is only for the brave. It is for those people who are willing to confront their pain, accept themselves as permanently changed, and make difficult choices. Countless individuals are satisfied to go on resenting and hating people who wrong them. They stew in their own inner poisons and even contaminate those around them. Forgivers, on the other hand, are not content to be stuck in a quagmire. They reject the possibility that the rest of their lives will be determined by the unjust and injurious acts of another person. Instead, people who forgive take risks to reshape their lives into something freed from past pain.[37]

Write it down:

- Each decision you make writes the next chapter in the story of your life. *If you choose to stay stuck what kind of story will be written? If you choose to make a heroic choice and forgive, what might your story look like in five, ten, twenty years?*

- *What are some factors keeping you from making a heroic choice?*

- *What can you do to overcome them?*

---

[37] *Forgiving the Unforgivable*, p. 71

Chapter Sixteen:

First Steps

I'm not much of a golfer. I play six times a year at most, but I've been playing for fifty years, so I've picked up a few tips along the way. One thing I've learned: the better I position myself, the better I hit the ball.

You don't just walk up to a ball and swing. You get yourself set: knees bent, back straight, hands slightly ahead of the ball, relaxed grip. When everything is in the right place, the chance of hitting the ball high and straight increases dramatically.

It's the same with forgiveness. Once you've made the *choice* to forgive, the next step is to *position* yourself to forgive. That's what I want to look at in the next three chapters: three steps you can take that will put you in the right position to forgive.

Don't Respond in Kind

To "respond in kind" means to do to others what they have done to you. I realize it's a natural response, but it only escalates the problem. When you respond in kind your offender feels obligated to do the same. That's how small disputes turn into all-out wars.

Have you ever noticed how we never pay back with equity? We always pay back, *plus one.* That's our way of saying, "If you mess with me, you'll be sorry."

Like I said before, you don't want to run to a fire with gas but water. The goal of your anger is not *revenge* but *resolution.* The Bible tells us:
> ...be like-minded, be sympathetic, love one another, and be compassionate and humble. Do not repay evil with evil or insult with insult. On the contrary, repay evil with blessing, because to this you were called so that you may inherit a blessing. For, "Whoever among you would love life and see good days must keep your tongue from evil and your lips from deceitful speech. Turn from evil and do good; seek peace and pursue it. For the eyes of the Lord are on the righteous and his ears are attentive to their prayer, but the face of the Lord is against those who do evil." 1 Peter 3:8-12

Peter uses Jesus as the best example of how to respond to an injustice. He says:
> When they hurled their insults at him, he did not retaliate; when he suffered, he made no threats. Instead, he entrusted himself to him who judges justly. 1 Peter 2:23

Peter teaches us a number of valuable insights in these two texts. First, we are *called* to bless others, even people who do evil to us. The word "called" is a strong word. It means God put us on earth for this purpose: to be a blessing to other people. To not bless is to forsake God's calling on our lives. Our calling isn't to merely *withhold* evil but to *offer* good.

Second, we are to *seek peace*, which means, *go looking for it.* When we find peace we are to *pursue* it: *to run after it until we catch it.* Peter charges his readers to go against their natural tendencies to be passive and work at reconciliation.

Third, Peter reminds his readers that *those who bless are blessed.* God's presence will be with them. There is compensation for giving up the right to get even.

Fourth, if they choose to *retaliate*, repaying evil with evil, then *God will be against them*. They may experience a momentary satisfaction from payback, but they will soon find God's presence is no longer with them.

Put simply, Peter tells people to not respond in kind (evil for evil). It's hard, but Jesus did it by trusting that God was in control, and we can too.

Write it down:
- *Be honest, how have you responded "in kind" to your offenders?*

- *Did it solve the problem? Did it escalate the problem?*

- *How can you seek peace with your offenders instead?*

- *If you have sought to bless your offenders, have you seen God bless you?*

- *If you have retaliated, have you seen any ways that God has been against you?*

Step Back and Reflect

There's nothing like being offended to give you a good look at your heart. But you will miss the opportunity if you are busy pointing the finger at your offender. If you want to "do good," as Peter suggests, then your next step is to evaluate your anger, and discover what has pushed your buttons.

Consider asking yourselves these questions about your anger:

What Is The Loss?
Whenever I sense I'm angry I always ask myself, *what is the loss?* My tendency is to just think I am irritable for no specific reason; it's the weather, or I'm tired, but there's always a deeper reason. For example, sometimes when my wife comes home she says hi to me, and I respond with an attitude, like I'm mad at her. It always surprises me (and her too). If I'm self-aware at the time, I'll stop and ask myself where the attitude came from. I'll think through my day to see if there were any losses that made me mad.

I can always pinpoint my anger to something; maybe I got a call from my mechanic telling me my $15 oil change just grew to $1200 after they inspected my car and found a few problems (true story). That's an $1185 loss I wasn't expecting. Ouch. My anger might sit all day beneath the surface and then pop its head up when my wife comes home. The quicker I can identify the source of my anger, the quicker I can deal with it and move on. I can also let my wife know why I'm so crabby and apologize to her.

On A Scale Of One To Ten, How Important Is The Loss?
Putting a number on the severity of my loss gives me perspective. Using my previous example, I may be upset I lost $1185, but I really gained a safer car for my family. If I have the money in the bank, it's simply a transfer of wealth: from my account to a safer car! Once I realize that, it's easier for me to release my anger. When I rate the loss at only a "2" (on a scale of one to ten), that helps me to calm down and let it go.

Is My Anger Appropriate Or Inappropriate?
It's easy to misread a situation and jump to conclusions. Then your emotion is totally out of line with reality. Maybe you are mad because you didn't get your way, or you misinterpreted something, or someone spoke the truth and it hurt. It takes humility to admit this, but you can nip a lot of anger in the bud by asking yourself this simple question. When your anger is obviously inappropriate it's a lot easier to drop it.

Who Is To Blame?

If you want to forgive it's important you know who's to blame. You may be reticent to assign blame, feeling you are judging others. Lewis Smedes writes:

> We do not excuse the person we forgive, we blame the person we forgive...we forgive people only for wounding and wronging us; we do not forgive people for things we do not blame them for...we cannot forgive a wrong unless we first blame the person who wronged us.[38]

When counseling I'll often ask people about their parents' impact on their lives. Sometimes they respond with, "I feel uncomfortable talking about them. They did their best." That may be true, but if they refuse to identify how their parents hurt them they'll never be able to forgive them for what they've done. Beverly Flanigan helps us here:

> Blaming means you assign responsibility to someone for causing an incident to happen and acknowledge the behavior is wrong... Blaming brings confusion into focus and clarifies who an injurer really is. It lets you know whom to forgive.[39]

Is There A Lie Associated With The Loss?

Sometimes we hold onto our anger because we feel like our offender has invalidated us. They may have intentionally invalidated us, or it may simply be perceived on our part. When that happens, we have to be careful not to believe lies about ourselves.

For example, you may not only be mad because you were laid off at work but because you believe the lie "I'll never measure up," or "I have no future." The primary loss is the layoff. That alone will make you angry. The secondary loss is the invalidation or at least the perceived invalidation. I talked about this earlier in the book.

Remember how important it is to have a good self-image if you want to forgive. The more lies you believe about yourself the more defensive you'll be toward your offender. Don't rush past this point. Take some time, get real honest with yourself, and identify the lies your offenses speak to you.

---

[38] *The Art of Forgiving*, p. 177-8
[39] *Forgiving the Unforgivable*, p.197

Asking these five questions will help you gain perspective on your loss.

Write it down:
- Practice asking yourself these questions by thinking of a recent loss.

- Now think of another example, and another. *Are there any patterns starting to develop? For example, after reflecting on your anger, is much of it appropriate or inappropriate? Are there similar lies that you find yourself believing?*

Set Boundaries

Sandy came into my office and slumped in her chair. "My life is going nowhere," she said. "Just when I think I'm getting ahead someone lets me down. I don't know why God does this to me. What's he got against me anyways?"

Sandy represents many people who feel stuck. She felt helpless and thwarted by God himself. In reality, God wasn't against Sandy as much as Sandy wasn't protecting herself from unwelcome guests. Sandy needed to develop boundaries and you might too.

It seems counter-intuitive. You'd think forgiveness means to draw close to someone. That's the hope, but in order to draw close, you might need to first create distance: find separation. It's hard to forgive someone if they are still offending you.

I counseled a couple once that not only had people actively offending them, but their offenders were inciting *other* people to offend them as well (mostly family members). I told this couple they needed to get some distance between themselves and their offenders, otherwise it would be too hard to forgive. If they kept listening to their family it would only drag them down.

You might be in a similar situation: continually offended by the same person in the same way. No matter how many times you confront them and forgive them they don't seem to get it. It's getting harder and harder to forgive them. They just keep hurting you over and over. What should you do? My advice for repeat offenders is to set boundaries.

Boundaries Offer Consequences

Setting boundaries is about having consequences for bad behavior. I'm not talking about punishing people. I'm talking about raising the level of consequence just enough to stop the offending behavior. I gave some examples of this earlier in the book.

People often ask, *"Are boundaries in the Bible?"* Let me give you a couple of examples. The first example is found in the book of Acts where the apostle Paul taught in a synagogue.

> Paul entered the synagogue and spoke boldly for three months, arguing persuasively about the kingdom of God. But some of them became obstinate; they refused to believe and publicly maligned the Way. So Paul left them. He took the disciples with him... Acts 19:8,9

Paul gave his heart and soul to these people every day for three months, but some people didn't respect him or his ministry. They trash-talked him. Finally, Paul said, "That's enough. I won't allow you to speak to me like this anymore." Then he took action to create space by leaving the synagogue. If you read the chapter you'll see that he rented space from a local school. Paul established a boundary between himself and his critics.

Another example of boundaries comes from Jesus. He sent his disciples off to spread his message and told them what to do if people rejected them:

> ... if any place will not welcome you or listen to you, shake the dust off your feet when you leave, as a testimony against them. Mark 6:11

In other words, don't bear their abuse, just move on to someone who cares about the message. Notice how shaking the dust off was "a testimony against them," that is, an accusation of their doing wrong. It's saying, *I came with good news from God, and you rejected me. You'll have to answer to God for this.* Jesus tells them it's okay to create separation between them and unhealthy people.

Are You Too Nice?

The reason we often have trouble forgiving is we allow people to keep offending us. We are too nice. Many of us justify it by saying we shouldn't judge, or we need to be kind, but that's typically just a cover for a fear of confrontation. Am I right? But it's better to say something out of love than be "nice" and have a heart full of hate toward someone. Sit your offender down and say:

> *What you are doing* (or saying) *is not okay. If you keep it up I'm going to find ways to put distance between us.*

You can soften this as much as is appropriate, but you get the idea. By being direct and creating space you actually make it easier to forgive. Here are a few metaphors for different types of boundaries you might need to put in place:

- **Velvet rope**: I'm thinking of those fancy ropes in theaters. They are more for show than serious crowd control. This is what you use with a reasonable person. All you have to do is tell them your concern, and they get it. They respect your space. Problem solved.
- **Picket fence**: A fence brings more definition than a rope. There are no gaps in the fence, but it's low and slatted: not too threatening. The fence makes it clear who you are, whom others are, and the separation you expect. Most people get the message: you want your space.
- **Eight-foot cement wall**: This is what is needed when people don't get the message. You tell them your boundaries, but they keep offending you anyway. So you make it almost impossible for them to offend you by building a large wall. They will have to work hard to get into your space.
- **Razor wire and guard towers**: This refers to creating the highest level of self-protection. Henry Cloud says that some people require,

"lawyers, guns and money" (with guns referring to police)[40]. It's the only way to get their attention and protect yourself from their invasive behavior. You no longer appeal to their good will or assume they will be reasonable. Their past behavior has proven they are untrustworthy and possibly evil. Since they can't be trusted, you unapologetically do whatever it takes to prevent them from hurting you.

This might seem harsh. It might not seem very "Christian." To the contrary, razor wire and guard towers give you the distance needed to be gracious. They give you the space to think clearly rather than lash back at people out of anger. The more people offend you, the more distance you need to create between the two of you.

For example, if you have a friend who insists on calling you late at night, ask them not to call after ten o'clock (velvet rope). If they keep calling, tell them you will no longer answer the phone after ten o'clock (picket fence). This provides a consequence that hopefully puts distance between you and ends the irritation.

But what if they persist and are a borderline stalker? When you don't answer the phone, they come over and knock on the door. Many people cave in at this point, welcome them in the house, and talk until they leave. Don't do this. Reaffirm your boundary. Tell them to go home, and should they choose to bother you again let them know you won't answer the door no matter how long they knock (concrete wall). In fact, you will consider calling the police (guard tower and razor wire).

This might strike you as over-the-top. You could never take these steps. But what happens inside of you when you fail to confront your offenders? You just get more and more mad. It becomes impossible to forgive. What you need are consequences to support your boundaries. Where there are no consequences there are no boundaries. Where there are no boundaries there will always be conflict, and conflict will be a continual source of anger to you.

---

[40] *Necessary Endings*

Take Back The Pens

Do you remember Sandy? The reason people like Sandy get so overwhelmed isn't because they have just one boundary breaker irritating them, they have a dozen or more. They just don't realize it. They have no idea how much energy they expend every day keeping their "friends" at bay or managing them as they tromp through their lives at will. No wonder they have trouble forgiving.

It's like having a number of people trying to "help" me write a book. They come with their own agenda, not interested in adding value to my writing. The only thing they add is confusion. If I let them continue, I will never finish my book. Or if I do, no one would buy it because it would make no sense. If there is any hope for my book, I need to stop these people from making their "contributions."

Is that what's happening in your life: you have a number of people making unwanted contributions? I encourage you to "take back the pens" from these "authors" (including family members). Your story should be written by God and the few people you trust to add value to your story. Too often we hand out pens to anyone who asks for one, letting them write a few paragraphs or even a chapter or two in our stories. That should never happen. You can control who writes your story.

Taking back the pens takes courage. People will get mad (especially family members), but you will start to enjoy life again once you reclaim control of your story.

Consequences, Not Punishment

One caution. Before you run off to set boundaries, be careful your boundaries consist of *consequences* and not *punishment*. For example, in my previous example, if you called the police the first time your friend came to your door it would be a punishment. The consequence doesn't match the offense. It will only infuriate the other person and cause things to escalate into hurt feelings. You may even lose the relationship. The goal isn't to cause an offense but to simply clarify the boundaries to help you get unstuck in a relationship. Inflaming the situation will only keep you stuck longer.

Write it down:

- *How much do you know about establishing healthy boundaries?*

- *If there are no consequences, you have no boundaries. What kind of consequences do people incur for crossing your boundaries?*

- *What kind of consequences (not punishment) can you develop to encourage people to comply with your boundaries?*

- *Are you punishing some people with your boundaries?*

Chapter Seventeen:

Reframing

In the book *Change or Die*, Alan Deutchman says there are three factors that contribute to change: relationships, retraining, and reframing. You need to have the right person coaching you (relationship), the right information (retraining), and to see your problem from a fresh perspective (reframing).

The Bible agrees with this assessment of the change process, especially when it comes to retraining and reframing. Romans 12:2 tells us to be "transformed by the renewing of your mind," and Ephesians 4:23 tells us to be "made new in the attitudes of your mind."

The apostle Paul took an aggressive approach to his thought life. He sees his mind as a battlefield:

> We demolish arguments and every pretension that sets itself up against the knowledge of God, and we take captive every thought to make it obedient to Christ. 2 Corinthians 10:5

This is what reframing is about. It's about taking your thoughts captive to serve you rather than allowing your thoughts to work against you.

In the next three chapters I want to help you reframe your situation by first reframing your offense, second reframing the outcome, and then reframing your identity. Reframing helps cast new light on your situation, empowering you to get unstuck.

Reframing the Offense

When you've been deeply hurt, the temptation is to turn your offender into the devil and polarize the situation into good and evil. By reframing your situation you can defuse this hostility. Here are two character traits that will enable you to reframe your offense.

Humility

Humility is the ability to see your own capacity to fail. The word comes from "humus," which means, "ground" referring to a modest attitude that is "low to the ground." It reminds us that we are all made from the dust of the earth and therefore fallible.

Lewis Smedes tells the story of a woman in a German prison camp who was forced to stand watch as a Nazi guard beat her friend. She was filled with rage and hatred toward this guard. Her mind spewed contempt for him and imagined the punishment he deserved. No sooner did she feel this contempt than a voice whispered in her mind, "Remember, there is also a Nazi in you."[41]

Remember, there is also a Nazi in you. Do you know what that means? It means, given the same situation as the Nazi, she may very well have turned out like he did. It means we all have the potential to do horrible

---

[41] As related by Gordon McDonald, *Ordering Your Private World*, (Thomas Nelson), p. 80

things, so be careful before you condemn someone for being evil.

This single caution from an internal voice reframed the offense and enabled the woman to release her anger. She realized that the seeds of evil were in her just like the Nazis. In the book, *To Forgive is Human*, the authors explain:

> Comprehending you are capable of the same ugliness you are condemning in another can penetrate a cloud of hatefulness. Have you ever been in the midst of an argument, your thoughts or your voice screaming condemnation at another because he or she doesn't care? "You do hateful things," you might be thinking. Or "You're insulting," you might say (insultingly). Or "You always put me down," you might say, putting the other person down. Suddenly, with the sharpness of a lightning flash, you realize your mind and mouth have betrayed you: you have the same flaws as the person who hurt you.[42]

You Are More Like Them Than You Care To Admit.

This ability to see you are capable of the same ugliness as your offender is what humility is about. It's what enables you to "penetrate a cloud of hatefulness." Whenever I catch myself judging another person I often ask myself, "Have you ever done what you are criticizing them of doing, or have you ever thought about doing it?" Nine times out of ten I have.

So then I ask myself, "Why are you so understanding of your own weakness and so judgmental when others do the same thing?" The authors I just quoted have an answer to that question. Let me quote them at length as they help us understand what is called the "fundamental attribution error."

> People tend to attribute their own negative behavior to circumstances beyond their control, (for example, finishing a project late because the boss gave him or her too much work) but attribute the negative behavior of others to something wrong with them (for example, he finished the project late because he is lazy). The fundamental attribution error

---

[42] *To Forgive is Human*, p. 62

suggests we are more willing to deny our own personal responsibility than we are to allow others to deny their responsibility.

This double standard of judging others in terms of their personalities while we judge ourselves in terms of the terrible circumstances we have suffered is pervasive.

It is not reasonable to explain the hurts we cause in terms of our circumstances while we explain the hurts others create as a function of their personalities. We cannot simply explain the sins of others against us by concluding they are brutes, monsters, unfeeling cowards or any other description, while we allow ourselves off the hook: "No one understands the kind of pressure I am under; if you had my childhood, you would have done the same thing."[43]

Now, listen to their conclusion:
> If we want to be people of integrity, we cannot allow ourselves to explain away our own failures while holding others responsible for theirs.[44]

The humble person refuses to do this. They own their ability to fail others in the same way that others have failed them.

There's a story in the Bible that reflects the *opposite* of humility. In the book of Mark, Jesus had just predicted that his disciples would betray him, and Peter proudly said:
> Even if all fall away, I will not. Mark 14:29

Peter was convinced he was incapable of betrayal. That was for lesser people. He was above that. Peter wasn't in touch with his own inner weakness. He didn't realize a Nazi lived inside of him. But if you read the story, Peter not only denied Jesus: *he denied Jesus three times.*

Peter lacked humility. Humility means you understand what it's like to

---

[43] Ibid. p. 30
[44] Ibid. p. 135

be desperately in need of forgiveness and therefore willing to offer it to others. A final quote from *To Forgive is Human* says:

> ...we recognize we stand in the same condition as our offenders. We have hurt others with our actions in the past and have also needed forgiveness.[45]

The Ferlaak Story

One of the most powerful stories of forgiveness I've heard is about Chip and Jody Ferlaak. Jody and Chip Ferlaak went to lunch after church with their three children (4, 2, infant). As they sat in the restaurant, a car going 70 mph hit the restaurant and came through the wall, right where they were sitting. The four year old died, the infant had multiple brain surgeries, and the two year old suffers from Post Traumatic Stress Disorder (PTSD), unable to sit at a table and eat haunted by the memory of the restaurant. The woman driving the car was attempting suicide.

Amazingly Jody and Chip were able to forgive the woman. A magazine article quotes Judy telling how she came to realize that there was not a lot of difference between the driver and her. She said:

> I was raised in a Christian family. I grew up with a dad who was a pastor and have known the love of Jesus my whole life. I could have been her, raised in a family where there's abuse and alcohol, [a place] where you know no love or hope.[46]

Then in an interview with Oprah Winfrey Jody told Oprah:

> As I sat at the scene of the accident, everyone was running around but I just sat there and looked at this woman. Over the weeks I would think about her, wondering, *What could have been going through her head? What could have caused her to do this?* And it's almost as though I heard a little voice inside saying, *You know what? Here's a woman. She's an average American woman, just like you. She grew up just a few blocks from where I was living at the time. It's not like her life was so different than mine.* So I kept thinking, *What is it that made her drive the car and do that where I was the one on the other*

---

[45] *To Forgive is Human*, p. 137
[46] Bethel Focus, Spring 2003

> *side of the wall?*
>
> There really wasn't a whole lot of difference between the two of us. And when you look at it that way that could have been me driving the car rather than her. You know, she could have been me. It just happened that I was born where I was.[47]

When Jody said, "there wasn't a whole lot of difference between the two of us...that could have been me driving the car..." she was reframing her offense with humility. Reframing set her free to forgive.

Write it down:
- *As you think about how you have been offended, do you think you could have done the same thing to others, given similar life situations or experiences?*

- *Can you see there could be "a Nazi in you?"*

- *What do you think about the Ferlaak's ability to forgive the driver that killed their daughter?*

Jody Ferlaak showed two qualities necessary for forgiveness: humility and empathy. Empathy is what I want to look at now.

Empathy
Research has shown that empathy contributes to our ability to forgive more than anything else.[48] I hope this fact grabs your attention and causes you to dial in to what I'm about to say.

Empathy has to do with understanding the woundedness of your offender. Empathy is closely related to humility. Humility helps you see how fallible *you* are. Empathy helps you see how fallible *others* are. Empathy doesn't excuse the offense, but it does help you to imagine

---
[47] *Oprah Winfrey Show*, August 22, 2002
[48] *Faces of Forgiveness*, p. 95

what it must be like to stand in the shoes of your offender and see what they see and feel what they feel. This is why the authors of *To Forgive is Human* tell us:

> Empathy is the plow that breaks up the hard ground of our hearts.[49]

When your wounded heart is softened, forgiveness can take root.

The best story to help me understand the power of empathy was told by Stephen Covey in his classic book, *Seven Habits of Highly Effective People*. Stephen was traveling on the city bus one day when a man boarded with what appeared to be his two sons. The man went to the back of the bus near Covey; he slumped in his seat and fell asleep. Meanwhile, the two boys ran about the bus, successfully annoying just about everyone on it.

Covey could see people's reactions and was starting to feel like it was his responsibility to say something to the man since he sat closest to him. Perturbed, Covey leaned over and tapped the man on the shoulder. The man rose from his slumber, and Covey said, "Excuse me sir, but your boys seem to be causing some trouble. Could you please bring them under control?" The man looked remorseful and said, "I'm so sorry. We just came from the hospital where their mother died this morning."

Listen to what Covey said about the man's response:

> Can you imagine how I felt at that moment? My paradigm shifted. Suddenly I saw things differently and because I saw things differently, I felt differently, I behaved differently. My irritation vanished. I didn't have to worry about controlling my attitude or my behavior. My heart was filled with the man's pain. Feelings of sympathy and compassion flowed freely. Everything changed in an instant.[50]

Wouldn't you like to have feelings of sympathy and compassion flow freely inside of you? That's the power of empathy. Empathy enables

---

[49] *To Forgive is Human*, p.223
[50] Stephen R. Covey, *Seven Habits of Highly Effective People: Powerful Lessons in Personal Change*, (Simon and Schuster), p. 31

you to reframe the offense in terms that help you better understand your offender.

Covey saw and felt the man's pain. He no longer saw the man as a terrible father. He saw him as a grieving husband of two grieving children, and it caused Covey to interpret the man's actions in a completely different way. The actions hadn't changed, but the *interpretation* of the actions was completely different, helping him to let go of his anger. It was as if he reconnected the dots and created a whole new picture from the same set of dots.

If you could understand your offender better, do you think you could forgive her or him? Chances are you would.

Reframing Abandonment

John Trent documents his own struggle with anger in his book, *How to Live the Blessing* and how reframing helped him overcome it. He tells the moving story of being raised in a home with just his mother and brother. His father had abandoned the family when John was very young. He said, surprisingly, he never felt a loss from his father's absence. His mother was a great parent, and he never knew life any other way, so it didn't bother him.

Then one day the phone rang. His mother answered; it was John's father. He had read about John and his younger brother being stars on the local football team, and it made him want to reconnect after many years. John's mom was reluctant, but she didn't think she could deny her boys the right to see their father so she set up a meeting after the Friday football game.

John tells how he had never thought about his father, but suddenly he was excited. He lived out fantasies in his mind of what it would be like to play catch with his dad in the back yard or go fishing in the mountains.

Friday finally came, and when the game was over the two boys and their mom went to the agreed upon location, at the bottom of the stadium, to meet their dad. As people streamed down the stadium stairs, John and his brother scrutinized each man to see if he might be the one. The stands finally emptied, and the lights were turned off. Their dad never showed. John was crushed.

Trent tells how that was a turning point in his life. He became an angry young man. He started to drink. He started to swear. He dated girls and purposefully dropped them without an explanation.

He went on to graduate from high school and then to college in Texas. One day he had to go to a different college library across town for research. As he walked out of the library he saw the librarian's office nameplate: Robert Trent. John said he had no idea what came over him, but he popped into the office and said, "Hi uncle Bob, I'm your long lost nephew." The man pushed back from his desk and asked John to come in.

It turned out the man wasn't his uncle, but he was his great uncle. Imagine the chances of that! He invited John to dinner that night where he explained to John how his dad fought in the Vietnam War and suffered post-traumatic stress disorder (PTSD) as a result of his tour of duty. When he came back to the United States, it was very hard for him to re-enter and live life in a normal way. That's why he abandoned his family. It was no excuse, but it was an explanation.

In reflecting back on that night John said it was at that moment his anger started to dissipate. His new found empathy for his dad enabled him to reframe the abandonment, and as a result forgiveness followed.

How To Gain Empathy

Both of these authors show us how hearing the story of your offender is a great asset in gaining empathy. The more you hear, the more you understand your similarities.

If you are want to better understand your offender, consider how you might learn more about their story. You might also try to engage in positive experiences with them: take a walk together, go to a movie, or enjoy a meal together. When you share a positive experience, you start to see they enjoy some of the same things you enjoy. It reveals they really are human and not the ogre you've made them out to be as you rehash events in your mind night after night. Of course, this isn't always possible if the offense was too great or your offender is no longer in your life. But for the offenders that still live under your roof, it's something to consider.

I spent extra time on this point because, as I mentioned before, empathy is *the most* powerful contributor to forgiveness. I hope you'll ask God to help you reframe your offender so you might find the power to forgive them.

Write it down:
- *How well do you know your offender? Do you know them well enough to understand why it is they hurt you?*

- *What can you do to better understand the heart of your offender? Is there someone to whom you can speak to gain an understanding of them?*

Reframing the Outcome

What often gets you stuck is not just being offended but where you end up as a result of the offense. For example, being fired is what offended you. Being unemployed is where you ended up as a result of getting fired. Getting divorced is what offended you. Being single again is the result. The death of your spouse is what offended you. Living as a widow is the result.

Humility and empathy help us reframe the *offense*. In the next two chapters I'll give you two ways to reframe the *outcome* of the offense.

Eliminate Expectations

At the beginning of the book I mentioned how anger results from unmet expectations. Therefore, the logical approach to eliminating anger is to simply eliminate your expectations. No expectations means:

no loss. No loss means: no anger. This isn't always possible, but let me give you a few examples of how it might help.

I discovered this truth way back in high school. My friends weren't the most reliable. They might tell me they were coming by to get me at 8:00 p.m. and not show up until 9:00 p.m. (We didn't have the luxury of minute by minute updates from cell phones back then). I would get mad at them for coming late, and it would often ruin the night when they finally did show up. So I decided to reframe the situation. I'd be ready at 8:00 p.m. but not expect them to come at all. That way, their arrival was a bonus. If other options came up after the appointed time, I felt free to take them. Of course, this didn't make for a trusting relationship, but it did help me with my anger and attitude once they picked me up.

Years later I tried this with my children, and it helped again. I noticed I had too many expectations of them. I thought they should be like little adults: able to make wise choices, thoughtful enough to replace every toy after they had gotten them out to play, etc. I was often upset about their behavior until I reframed the outcome. I still held goals for wisdom and thoughtfulness to prevail, but I was no longer angry when it didn't happen.

Die To Yourself

Eliminating expectations is another way of talking about "dying to self." I looked at this earlier when I talked about dying to your expectation for respect. Let's explore this a little more. Jesus said:

> Unless a grain of wheat falls into the ground and dies, it remains alone. But if it dies, it will produce a large crop. John 12:24

Jesus used this analogy to explain a common principle of his; death precedes life. Before you can obtain what you desire you need to give it up first.

This means that sometimes God wants you to die to your expectations because they are keeping you back from what he has in store for you. That's when you can truly start to live. If you insist on your expectations becoming reality, you may "remain alone," that is, unproductive, while the rest of your fellow "seedlings" (other people) sprout, grow and produce fruit.

Sometimes, the correct response to anger is to resolve injustice. Other times God says (paraphrasing John 12:24):
> *Let your expectations go. You took a loss. You've been hurt. You've complained and grieved. To hold onto it any longer is counter-productive. It's time to let it go or you will remain alone (stuck). When you let go, you will get your life back and you will prosper.*

For example, let's say a loved one died at a young age, and you are still angry. It's not right. Why would God take such a young woman, in the prime of her life, leaving behind three children and a husband? Those are all valid feelings, thoughts, and questions to have. But at some point you need to say, "I release my expectation that all people must live a long life and die quietly in their sleep. That's not a realistic expectation." Or let's say someone betrayed you. At some point it's important to say, "I'm going to release my expectation that everyone on the planet will treat me with dignity and respect, always concerned about my feelings."

The New Testament message is that we ought to die to our expectations and humbly accept what life has dealt us. Jesus made it plain what kind of followers he wanted:
> Whoever wants to be my disciple must deny themselves and take up their cross and follow me. Matthew 16:24

To deny yourself and take up your cross means you let go of your expectations on life and trust that what God has for you will be good. The apostle Paul embraced this metaphor for his life by saying:
> I have been crucified with Christ and I no longer live, but Christ lives in me. Galatians 2:20

Paul tells us that dead men don't have expectations. Dead men aren't disappointed. Dead men can't be offended. When you die to *your* wants and desires then God can breathe *his* wants and desires into you. Therefore dead men are able to forgive because they aren't consumed with what they want. They are free to pursue what God wants.

Paul wrote to a church in Greece, reproving them for their inability to get along with each other. It had gotten so bad they were suing each other in court. This was embarrassing to Paul. He said:

> To have such lawsuits at all is a real defeat for you. Why not just accept the injustice and leave it at that? Why not let yourselves be cheated? 1 Corinthians 6:7

Paul told them their lawsuits came from expectations that didn't have to be met. He called on the church to reframe their situation. Instead of insisting every wrong must be set right, they should be willing to reframe the story and let it end unresolved with them bearing a loss. It's a much better end to the story than having fellow believers sue each other in court and give the church a bad name.

You can't eliminate all expectations, but many expectations are unnecessary: even bad for you. If you hold them loosely you might find forgiveness isn't even necessary because no loss was incurred, and no anger resulted in the first place.

A Word Of Caution

There are so many exceptions when it comes to broken relationships. I find that there are two kinds of people: people that are quick to fight for their rights and people that are quick to give in. My experience is that God often tells powerful people to die to their rights while he often tells weaker people to fight for their rights.

I mention this because I'm afraid people often hear the message meant for someone else. When I talk about giving up your rights and denying yourself, the downtrodden are often quick to take that on while the powerful are deaf to it. On the other had, when God wants to encourage people to stand up for their rights, the powerful people are the ones who hear that message while the weak don't think it's for them. So, be careful to assess what message God is speaking to you.

Write it down:

- *How would you answer Paul? Why should you let yourself be cheated?*

- *What are some expectations you have in life that are unnecessary and only cause you to get angry?*

- *How can you reframe your expectations to see your losses in a positive role?*

- *Do you consider yourself a weak person who needs to learn how to stand up for your rights or a powerful person who needs to relinquish your rights?*

Look for the Silver Lining

Another way to re-frame the result of an offense is to see the silver lining that often follows a loss.

I'll never forget the time I taught this point at the treatment center. I was going on about how it's easier to forgive when you see something good come out of your loss.

For example, I talked about a time in my life that was very hard for me. It was hard physically, emotionally and financially. I worked harder than I had ever worked for less money than I had ever earned. But those years helped me to be a more empathic counselor and pastor. I told people the silver lining for me was, had I not gone through hard times, I wouldn't be able to relate to people and their pain as I counsel them.

There were five women in my group of seven, and all five of them revealed they had been raped, so they weren't buying this "silver lining" idea. As I thought how to answer them the 9/11 tragedy popped into my mind, and I said:

> I can see what you are saying. That's fair. I don't want to minimize what happened to you in any way. Hold your thoughts, and let's do a little exercise. When terrorists hit the Twin Towers, over three thousand people died, countless

families were traumatized, and our nation suffered an incredible hit below the belt. With all that considered, did anything good come out of it?

Everyone seemed to shift gears and immediately started listing off good things: victim's families grew closer, people poured out love by way of money and thoughtful care, people flew across the country to help, homeland security suddenly became a nationwide concern, patriotism soared, many people decided to slow down and pay more attention to their families, and so on.

After ten minutes of writing down these ideas I stopped and said, "Do you see what just happened? When we looked into someone else's tragedy, it was easy to see the silver lining. 9/11 was the greatest homeland attack in America's history. Yet, we found a silver lining. That's not to say it was 'worth it', but something good came from it. Is it possible that there might be a silver lining in your life too?"

You could see the light break across these women as they considered, probably for the first time, that something good could come out of something evil. Re-framing didn't justify what happened to them, but it helped to recast evil in a positive light. When given to God, even evil can be transformed into good.

Isn't this what's at the heart of the Jesus story? God took the most evil thing imaginable, the crucifixion of his Son, and used it for good. The key to overcoming evil is staying around for the resurrection. Don't leave before the stone is rolled away. That is, don't give up on your life when bad things happen. God is a god of resurrection; so wait for it.

Jesus' story stands as a word of hope for every victim of abuse. As terrible as rape is, wouldn't it reveal the transforming power of God if these five women could find forgiveness for their offenders, healing for their emotional wounds, and wisdom to help other victims do the same? Who better to minister to other victims than women who have found the healing grace of God?

The apostle Paul often re-framed his circumstances to see the good in what happened to him. For example, he wrote a letter while he was in prison. He didn't focus on what was wrong but what was right.

Imagine his situation. Roman prisons were rat-infested dungeons with slop for food. No running water. No bathrooms. No cafeteria. No human rights laws. Most prisoners would send a letter home asking for help or sympathy and filled with complaints, but Paul says:

> Now I want you to know, brothers and sisters, that what has happened to me has actually served to advance the gospel. As a result, it has become clear throughout the whole palace guard and to everyone else that I am in chains for Christ. And because of my chains, most of the brothers and sisters have become confident in the Lord and dare all the more to proclaim the Gospel without fear. Philippians 1:12-14

Paul was able to look at his suffering and see only the good of what God was doing. God was using his imprisonment to advance God's message to the world. Paul continues with gracious comments about other ministers who act with less than noble motives:

> It is true that some preach Christ out of envy and rivalry, but others out of goodwill. The latter do so out of love, knowing that I am put here for the defense of the Gospel. The former preach Christ out of selfish ambition, not sincerely, supposing that they can stir up trouble for me while I am in chains. But what does it matter? The important thing is that in every way, whether from false motives or true, Christ is preached. And because of this I rejoice. Yes, and I will continue to rejoice... Philippians 1:12-18

Some people would go on a crusade against these unethical preachers and try to purge them from the church but not Paul. They didn't offend him. He chose to see the good in how even these misguided preachers were being used to tell the story of God's love. Paul re-framed his situation. He was able to rise 30,000 feet in the air and look down on his imprisonment from God's point of view. Because of that, he rejoiced.

The Gift Of Pain

If you are able to see the silver lining in your pain, you might even be able to see pain as a gift. It's a sign of deep maturity but not uncommon among people who know God.

The apostle Paul understood this. He wrote to a church in Greece:
> Praise be to the God and Father of our Lord Jesus Christ, the Father of compassion and the God of all comfort, who comforts us in all our troubles, so that we can comfort those in any trouble with the comfort we ourselves have received from God. 2 Corinthians 1:3-5

Paul wasn't talking theory here. He knew trouble first hand: often facing death, starvation, persecution, and more. But he was able to reframe pain to see it as a gift and still praise God for his life.
> If we are distressed, it is for your comfort and salvation; if we are comforted, it is for your comfort... 2 Corinthians 1:6

This is not normal thinking! It's like a friend feeling sorry for your situation, and you tell them...*Oh. Yes...I suppose it is bad news for me, but it's good news for you because I'll be able to comfort you better when you go through hard times.* Who does that?

That's what I mean by the gift of pain. I'm not talking about denying your reality, slapping on a plastic smile, or over spiritualizing your loss. I never like it when people think this behavior pleases God. Paul was able to sincerely see the good in his suffering. He was willing to endure suffering if it helped others and honored God.

Pain Is Our Teacher

Pain is able to teach you what nothing else can. What class do you sign up for to learn humility, empathy, compassion, patience, or faith? No college offers this degree. Yet that's what pain teaches you if you are willing to learn.

Pain causes us to cry out to God. The Bible tells us God is close to those who are crushed in spirit. I want to quote for you most of Psalm 31 so you can hear firsthand from someone who knew God and experienced God in the depth of his suffering. This is a song written by David, the one I told a few stories about earlier in the book.
> In you, LORD, I have taken refuge; let me never be put to shame; deliver me in your righteousness. Turn your ear to me;

come quickly to my rescue; be my rock of refuge, a strong fortress to save me. Since you are my rock and my fortress, for the sake of your name lead and guide me. Keep me free from the trap that is set for me, for you are my refuge. Into your hands I commit my spirit; redeem me, LORD, my faithful God.

I will be glad and rejoice in your love, for you saw my affliction and knew the anguish of my soul. You have not given me into the hands of the enemy but have set my feet in a spacious place.

Be merciful to me, LORD, for I am in distress; my eyes grow weak with sorrow, my soul and body with grief. My life is consumed by anguish and my years by groaning; my strength fails because of my affliction, and my bones grow weak. Because of all my enemies, I am the utter contempt of my neighbors; I am a dread to my friends-- those who see me on the street flee from me. I am forgotten as though I were dead; I have become like broken pottery. For I hear many whispering, "Terror on every side!" They conspire against me and plot to take my life.

But I trust in you, LORD; I say, "You are my God." My times are in your hands; deliver me from the hands of my enemies, from those who pursue me. Let your face shine on your servant; save me in your unfailing love.

How great is your goodness, which you have stored up for those who fear you, which you bestow in the sight of all on those who take refuge in you. In the shelter of your presence you hide them from all human intrigues; you keep them safe in your dwelling from accusing tongues.

Praise be to the LORD, for he showed me the wonders of his love when I was in a city under siege. In my alarm I said, "I am cut off from your sight!" Yet you heard my cry for mercy when I called to you for help. Love the LORD, all his faithful people! The LORD preserves those who are true to him, but the proud he pays back in full. Be strong and take heart, all you who hope in the LORD.

I love this psalm because it shows the full breadth of our humanity. David was fully honest about his dark place in life, yet fully hopeful in what God could do. He didn't give up on life or God because he was in a bad place. He used his distress to draw closer to God.

Did you see the verse that said God showed David the wonders of his love *when he was in a city under siege*? That's amazing. It was when he was under a full attack from his enemy that the revelation of God's love came to David. Surprisingly, suffering can bring you an intimacy with God you can rarely find when life is "good." Pain allows God to work something deep in you so he can use it to benefit others.

Wounded Healers

Character, wisdom, and intimacy with God often come as a result of a gift of pain. Consider an abuse victim for example. I mentioned earlier about the rape victims I counseled. Maybe you are also a victim of some kind of abuse. If you've been abused, you know something many don't know. You know a side to life many haven't seen or experienced. You have a choice as to how you will treat that knowledge. You can resent the knowledge and focus on what has been stolen from you, living the life of a victim. Or you can view your knowledge as a gift to help others in pain.

Yes, something has been taken from you, but something has also been given. The question is, do you want to use what you've been given to help others? Or will you choose to throw away everything associated with the abuse and call it all bad?

Imagine I've been abused, and I'm looking to talk to someone. If I have the choice of talking to you (the abused) or talking to someone who hasn't been abused, with whom will I want to speak? I'll want to speak to you, without a doubt. Why? Because you have something the other person doesn't have. I don't look at you as deficient or handicapped. I look at you as rich in experience and wisdom: a great resource to my pain. What you have is *priceless*.

This is both ironic and possibly offensive. It's ironic because who would ever think the result of abuse could be priceless? It could also be offensive because you may not want to assess any value to something that was stolen from you. In fact, you might say, *I don't want to be a great resource. I never asked for this. I don't care if you think it's priceless. I don't want to have anything to do with it.*

I understand that, but you can't unscramble the eggs. You can't change your situation. You can either let the abuse haunt you and continue to steal from you for life, or you can re-frame what's happened to you, overcome it, and let God turn what was meant for evil into something good.

You've earned your wisdom. You paid a great price for it, so why would you want to waste it? It's like going to medical school and working in a factory. That's exactly what happens with so many people. They go through hard times then waste the experience. They hunker down, pull the sheet up over their heads, hold their breath, and ride it out: praying to God they'll survive. When the pain is over, they want to bury any memory of it; act like it never happened. They put as much distance between themselves and their pain as they possibly can. Or they play the victim, spend their life complaining, and seek out sympathy.

However, if they can accept it, they've been given a gift...the gift of pain. Imagine the good that could come if they would share their wisdom with those who have suffered like they have.

Write it down:

- *How does it feel to consider there might be a silver lining to your pain?* It might involve conflicting feelings of both resentment and hope. Explore your feelings about this.

- Consider other people who have experienced loss. *Can you see any silver lining in what they experienced?*

- *How have some people overcome their pain and others let it overcome them? Which is happening in your life right now?*

What do you want to happen?

- *What do you need to do to make sure you overcome your pain?*

Re-framing Your Identity

We are fragile beings. We can be full of confidence and hope one minute and an emotional wreck the next. If we perform well and people like us, we feel great. If we experience failure and people show disappointment in us, we despair.

How you view your identity has a lot to do with your ability to forgive. The more secure you are, the more easily you forgive. Here are two ways to re-frame your identity.

1. Differentiate Yourself

To be differentiated means you are able to separate your identity from another person; you see yourself as separate or "different." It is the opposite of being co-dependent. The undifferentiated person doesn't know where they stop and another person begins. They depend on someone else for their sense of self. When they get hurt they need another person to affirm them. Plus they find it hard to make decisions without the input of another person because they never feel adequate all by themselves.

An example might help. Imagine I'm undifferentiated and you are my close friend. When you offend me it feels like a betrayal. *How could you do this to me? Don't you realize I need you? I can't live without your affirmation!* I'm in crisis, and you put me there. But what really hurts is that I've got nowhere to turn. By you offending me, it's now twice as hard to forgive because you are the one I trust to save me.

But if I'm able to differentiate myself from you, I realize I have value and identity *apart* from you. I am a whole person. Your invalidation hurts, but it doesn't paralyze me. I can go on with my life feeling valuable because I don't depend on your affirmation.

How I respond to your offense is a matter of how I frame my world. When I look in the mirror, whom do I see? Do I see half a person who needs others to make me complete? Or do I see a whole person who can benefit from others but is not dependent on them?

Studies have shown that people who are able to differentiate themselves from their offender are much more likely to forgive.[51] They are able to sift out the personal insult from the offense, which in turn declaws it. It takes the power out of the punch and makes it manageable. Rather than devastating them, it merely rocks them momentarily. They are able to steady themselves and move on.

How To Find Your True Identity.

I believe the best way to differentiate yourself is to find your identity in God. Jesus made it clear to people where he found his worth. He said:
> If I give honor to myself, that honor is worth nothing. The One who gives me honor is my Father... John 8:54 NCV

Jesus didn't look to others for affirmation or identity. His worth came from God. Jesus chided the people of his day on this point saying:
> How can you believe since you accept glory from one another, but do not seek the glory that comes from the only God? John 5:44

He said people were mistaken to find their worth in other people and not in God. In another place he said:
> What shall I say about the people of this time? What are they like? They are like children sitting in the marketplace, calling to one another and saying, "We played music for you, but you did not dance; we sang a sad song, but you did not cry." Luke 7:31,32

Jesus' words are a bit cryptic, but what he meant is he didn't dance to the tune of any person. People complained about him not responding to them the way they wanted him to respond. But Jesus was not driven to please others, only God. Jesus was fully differentiated and so he was

---

[51] *Faces of Forgiveness*, pp. 50-62

able to follow his own calling without being bullied or intimidated by others who wanted him to play their game. His goal was never to keep people happy, so when they rejected him, it wasn't devastating. That is why, even in his death, he was able to say, "Father forgive them for they do not know what they are doing." Luke 23:34

Write it down:
- *Based on my definition, would say you are differentiated from other people?*

- *If not, to whom are you dependent for a sense of worth?*

- *How can you begin to separate yourself from this dependence?*

- *How do you think being differentiated would help you in your relationships and specifically in your ability to forgive others?*

2. Develop An Abundance Mentality

My last recommendation for re-framing has to do with choosing to see God as a god of abundance, not scarcity. I spoke about this briefly during my discussion of the Grief Cycle. You choose what glasses you put on each morning to view your world. Will you look at life expecting God to show up in a big way? Or will you assume the worst?

Scarcity is about fear. You are afraid there won't be enough for you: enough money, enough love, enough time, enough forgiveness: whatever it is you feel you need in life. Scarcity focuses on what little you have; it's all you'll get, and if you aren't careful you will even lose that. Scarcity is about walls and locks and secrets and hiding because you can never be too careful to guard your meager holdings.

Abundance is the opposite. Abundance is about hope. Abundance always sees the opportunities. I'm looking out the window right now at all the maple tree "helicopter" seeds falling to the ground. One tree throws off thousands of seeds. One tree could create a forest. God has wired abundance into his creation if we will only see it.

I don't think you have to believe in God to have an abundance mentality. You just need to see that abundance and opportunity exists. Believing in God helps because God can create something out of nothing. Even when all hope is seemingly lost, God has a way of bringing things into existence, i.e. think resurrection.

Two Spies

There are many stories in the Bible that reflect an abundance mentality. One that stands out is the story of the ten spies that scouted out the Promised Land. God had just brought his people out of bondage in Egypt. Only eleven days later God tells Moses to send spies into the new Land. These spies were meant to act as leaders. They were supposed to come back to the people and tell them the challenges, but their God was bigger than the challenges!

Two spies understood their calling. They said:
> "We went into the land to which you sent us, and it does flow with milk and honey! Here is its fruit. But the people who live there are powerful, and the cities are fortified and very large. We even saw descendants of Anak there (meaning, giants). The Amalekites live in the Negev; the Hittites, Jebusites and Amorites live in the hill country; and the Canaanites live near the sea and along the Jordan (full of enemies)." Then Caleb silenced the people before Moses and said, "We should go up and take possession of the land, for we can certainly do it!" Numbers 13:27-30

Joshua and Caleb were able to re-frame the situation. The land was fully occupied with other tribes, even giants, but they were convinced their God was bigger than anything the Promised Land could throw at them. They had an abundance mentality.

The remaining spies weren't so optimistic. They said:
> "We can't attack those people; they are stronger than we are." They spread among the Israelites a bad report about the land

> they had explored. They said, "The land we explored devours those living in it. All the people we saw there are of great size. We saw the Nephilim there ... We seemed like grasshoppers in our own eyes, and we looked the same to them." Numbers 13:27-30

Their report had a big impact on the people. The people all wanted to rebel against Moses and return to Egpyt! The story continues:

> Then Moses and Aaron fell facedown in front of the whole Israelite assembly gathered there. Joshua, son of Nun, and Caleb, son of Jephunneh, who were among those who had explored the land, tore their clothes and said to the entire Israelite assembly, "The land we passed through and explored is exceedingly good. If the LORD is pleased with us, he will lead us into that land, a land flowing with milk and honey, and will give it to us. Only do not rebel against the LORD. And do not be afraid of the people of the land, because we will devour them. Their protection is gone, but the LORD is with us. Do not be afraid of them." But the whole assembly talked about stoning them. Numbers 14:5-10

This story seems so relevant to me personally. How many times have I stood on the brink of something good, only wanting to go back to the "good old days" that are safe and comfortable? I've wanted to "stone" what God had for me. Even more convicting is how God responded to the people's rebellion:

> How long will these people treat me with contempt? How long will they refuse to believe in me, in spite of all the signs I have performed among them? Numbers 14:11

When I have a scarcity mindset I hold God in contempt. I tell him he's not enough. He is not sufficient for my need.

Paraphrasing, God says, *Okay. It's your choice. If you don't think I can help you overcome the obstacles then fine, don't enter the Promised Land.* And in fact, they didn't enter. They wandered in the Sinai Peninsula for forty years. You could say they were stuck, but it didn't have to be that way.

God's Grace Is Sufficient

When you look at your life, are you stuck simply because you refuse to believe in God's goodness and power? Again, the apostle Paul had a knack for re-framing his identity. When he was confronted with his weakness, he didn't despair and give up. Paul relates what God spoke to him along with his own response:

> "My grace is sufficient for you, for my power is made perfect in weakness." Therefore I will boast all the more gladly about my weaknesses, so that Christ's power may rest on me. That is why, for Christ's sake, I delight in weaknesses, in insults, in hardships, in persecutions, in difficulties. For when I am weak, then I am strong. 2 Corinthians 12:9-10

My point in this section on re-framing is that your ability to forgive and move on in life has a lot to do with how you choose to see the offense, how you see the result of the offense, and how you see your own identity. God has done everything necessary for you to overcome the worst offense, but it requires that you choose well, and then act on your choice.

Write it down:

- *Would you say you have an abundance mentality or a scarcity mentality? Are you more like Joshua and Caleb or the Israelites?*

- *How has it impacted you?*

- *What will it take to switch to an abundance mentality?*

Forgiveness Trivia:

Research shows that after four hours of training on forgiveness, people are less motivated to forgive than when they started. That is, most people approach the idea of forgiveness believing it's the right thing to do but think it's easier than it really is. The more they learn about forgiveness, the more discouraged they become!

But if they hang in there, research also shows they regain hope after the fifth and sixth hour. It all starts to make sense. The pieces fall into place, and they believe it's worth trying. In fact, the research shows that the more exposure you have to forgiveness training the more likely you are to forgive.[52]

So don't quit now! Push through the overwhelming sense of "I can never do this," and you'll find you truly can forgive and get unstuck. Then, beyond this book, keep reading on the topic. You will slowly wear down your resistance and forgiveness will eventually become a habit.

---

[52] *Forgiveness: Theory Research and Practice*, (Guilford Press) pp. 235-6

Part Three

Practical Steps

If you've made it this far in the book, you have thought through some of the tougher emotional barriers to remaining stuck. Hopefully you are ready to roll up your sleeves and move from thinking to taking action.

Here is some practical advice to help you move toward forgiveness.

1. Develop a Support System

Processing anger and repairing broken relationships is hard work. Like any hard work, it's nice to have help. To get the help you need I have two suggestions: get a counselor and find a support group.

Find A Good Counselor

Do you know how John Kennedy Jr. died (the son of President Kennedy)? He was flying a small plane, and it crashed in the ocean. When investigators got the black box out of Kennedy's plane, they found that his instruments were fine; it wasn't an instrument malfunction. It was probably pilot error.

Some people suspect vertigo. Vertigo is the sensation where you lose your physical bearings; you can even lose the sense of what's up and down. It's possible, since he was traveling at dusk, that Kennedy lost track of what was up and what was down on the horizon: which was sky and which was ocean. Because of that, some suspect his plane made a slow roll without him knowing it. If he went with his feelings and not his instrument panel, he may have crashed into the ocean when he intended on climbing in elevation. By the time he understood what was happening, it was too late.

This tragedy didn't have to happen. It was preventable.

Unresolved anger is like emotional vertigo. It can cause you to lose your bearings and misread what would seem obvious under normal conditions. Unfortunately, many people crash-land in life due to the bad decisions they make in the heat of their anger. Counselor Gary Collins says:
> Because we feel vulnerable, threatened or inclined to be critical, we misperceive the actions of others and jump to angry, perhaps unjustified conclusions.[53]

That's why it's so important to include a reliable, experienced person in your anger process to keep you accountable to the truth. They are like a pilot's instrument panel monitoring your status. I like this description of a good counselor:

---

[53] Gary R. Collins, *Psychology & Theology: Prospects for integration* (1981)

> The person you choose to talk to should be patient, wise, non-judgmental, and not afraid of your emotions – whether they are emotions of grief and pain or hate and rage. A good listener is also respectful of your perceptions of the injury. Avoid someone who challenges or invalidates your experiences.[54]

This last sentence is important and separates the average counselor from the excellent. Your emotions and experiences may be off base and questionable, but they are real *to you*. It's imperative you find someone who will listen to what you think, feel, and experience without saying you are necessarily wrong. You don't want to filter what you're saying to your counselor just to avoid their negative reaction. They should be there for *you*, not the other way around.

For example, if I panic whenever I smell lilacs, that is definitely a sign of a problem, but it's not wrong. It doesn't help for someone to tell me, "It's just your imagination" or "Don't worry about it. It's no big deal." As illogical as my fear may be, it's still very real to me. I need my counselor to help me process my experience, not minimize or dismiss it.

Find an objective friend or wise counselor who can help you walk through the minefield of anger. A general rule of thumb is: the more emotional the issue, and the higher the stakes involved in the decision, the more important it is to incorporate a proven counselor. You don't want to make life-altering decisions on your own, especially while you are under the influence of anger.

Find A Support Group

Besides finding a wise counselor, join a positive support group. Since God wired you for relationship he will often use other people to encourage you when you are on the verge of giving up. Like ineffective counselors, you will find groups that don't help. They spend their time talking about trivial matters, gossiping, or offering unsolicited advice. Stay away from groups like this. Find groups that stick to a program, accept you unconditionally, and are bold enough to challenge your

---

[54] *Forgiving the Unforgivable*, p. 184

thinking without being controlling or invasive.

There are a number of church-based groups that you might want to consider. One is *Celebrate Recovery*: for recovering addicts. Another is *DivorceCare*: for people rebuilding their lives after divorce. There is also *GriefShare*: which helps people process their grief. These are all national groups. You can probably find a church in your area offering one of these groups or something similar.

Another support group that might help is a church: *a healthy one*. This might sound odd coming from a pastor, but be careful in selecting a church. Don't assume any church you stumble into is healthy. When you look for a doctor or dentist you don't visit the closest one to your house or the one with the slickest ad, right? Most people ask their friends for a recommendation. There are some bad doctors and dentists out there. Unfortunately, there are some bad churches too: churches that will not help you get unstuck or closer to God. If you look long and hard enough, you will find the diamonds that will accept you unconditionally and help you find God's power to change. Don't stop until you find a church like that.

Write it down:
- *Who do you know that you would trust to help guide you through the forgiveness process?*

- *Who can you ask for a recommendation for a counselor, group, or church?*

- *What support groups are you aware of that you could join?*

- *Are you in a healthy church? If it's unhealthy, what effect might that be having on you?*

2. List Positive Attributes
The next practical step is to write out your offender's positive

attributes. I realize in the case of extreme offenses, let's say a rape, this might not be possible: especially if you don't know anything about the offender. However, in most of our relational breakdowns, we deal with people who have at least some redeemable qualities.

As I said before, we tend to label people as "all bad" when they've hurt us, so this step brings some balance to the picture of your offender. Sit down with a piece of paper, and ask God to show you their good qualities. If you still have a blank sheet of paper after this exercise, talk to mutual friends whom you know like this person. Tell them what you are doing: searching for their positive attributes to help you forgive them. Just be careful not to use this as an opportunity to tell people what a bad person he or she is. Don't go to your friends unless you can do it with a reasonably sincere and pure heart.

You might not find anything positive about your offender, but there are some positive attributes that are true of everyone. Write these things down and meditate on them.
> *God created your offender.*
> *God loves them.*
> *God has a plan for their life.*
> *God forgives them.*
> *God wants to transform them into the image of Jesus.*

Once again, use the art of re-framing your perception to see your offender from God's perspective. As your perspective changes you'll find it easier to forgive.

3. Write Out Your Feelings
I heard this story about Abraham Lincoln's secretary of war, Ed Stanton.

> An army officer who accused him of favoritism angered Stanton. Stanton complained to Lincoln, who suggested to Stanton that he write the officer a sharp letter. Stanton did, and showed the strongly worded letter to the President. "What are you going to do with it?" Lincoln inquired. Surprised, Stanton replied, "Send it." Lincoln shook his head. "You don't want to send that letter. Put it in the stove. That's

what I do when I have written a letter while I am angry. It's a good letter and you had a good time writing it and feel better. Now burn it, and write another one."[55]

Isn't that great advice? I wish someone had given me that advice thirty years ago. It would have saved me a lot of embarrassment.

For example, I once wrote a strong letter to a former business partner who reneged on his word regarding our business. I asked my wife to read it through to see if it was appropriate. She said it was worded strongly and he might get mad. I said, "Well, I don't care. I'm mad, and I want him to know it." (Not one of my finer moments).

A few months later, another businessperson let me down in a significant way. I wrote a letter telling him how I felt. Again, I asked my wife to read the letter, and again she said it was inflammatory and might cause offense. Sensing a trend, I thought I should listen this time (what a concept!). I let the letter sit for a few days, reread it, and was amazed how many inflammatory words and phrases I had used, things like: "you never do this" or "you always do that."

I edited out all the negative words in my letter and was about to send it but then thought, *You know, two days ago, I believed this was a great letter. Maybe this letter is still too harsh. I better wait two more days.* So, I did wait, and guess what? I found even more inflammatory words two days later. I was shocked, but it taught me a valuable lesson about the power of anger. Anger distorts my thinking, and so I need to be in a good place before I make any important decisions (or write any letters).

My point is: writing out your feelings is a great way to blow off steam as well as analyze your thinking. As long as your thoughts are locked in your brain, you tend to think they are better than they really are, but you can't deny what's written on paper. It's all there in black and white.

Author and counselor Larry Crabb once said half of all problems are solved just by telling them to somebody. There's just something about

---

[55] *Today in the World*, Feb. 1991

getting the offense out of your brain and into the open that diminishes its effect on you. It's one reason journaling is so helpful and why I've been giving you opportunities to "write it down" throughout this book.

When you write out your feelings, you'll be surprised how much your anger starts to diminish.

Write it down:
- Take time to write out your feelings in a "no-send" letter to someone who has offended you. Wait a few days, and then review what you wrote. I think you will be surprised at what you learn from this exercise. Hopefully, it will teach you to slow down and critique all your communication when you are angry.

Chapter Eighteen:

Having the Conversation

Before I entered the ministry for the second time (I took a number of years off after my initial run at ministry), I wanted to enter with a clean slate. I didn't want to bring any baggage into my ministry that might cause me to be less effective in any way.

I sat down and asked God to show me anyone from my past with whom I might be at odds. Thankfully, there wasn't a long list to clean up, but one name was obvious. It was a partnership that broke down dramatically several years ago, and I knew what I had to do.

I called this former partner and invited him to dinner. He was pleasant and agreed to the meeting. When the evening came, we had a nice dinner and caught up on the past seven years. We had been good friends until a breach took place, so I enjoyed reconnecting. I was hopeful we could renew our relationship.

I wasn't content to merely get reacquainted. I believed God wanted more from me, so I broached the subject of our parting. I said, "You know, I'm sorry it worked out the way it did. I'm sure we both did things wrong, and I'd like to talk about it. Maybe we can get together again and talk it through."

At this point his mood changed. It was like a chill came into the room. His responses were curt, and you could tell he was ready to go home. I got him to agree to meet again, but I felt it was in word only. The minute he walked out the door he had no intention of seeing me again.

At first I was confused by what happened. Everything seemed to be going so well. Then it dawned on me; my former partner was so positive about our meeting because he was sure I was going to apologize for our fractured relationship. He didn't feel any responsibility for what happened. It was all on me. No wonder the air got so cold when I suggested otherwise.

I didn't understand why God would bring this man to mind when it ended so poorly. But then I realized there was value in having our conversation even though it didn't end in reconciliation. I was able to forgive him and bring closure to our relationship, even though he rejected me. As I noted before, forgiveness isn't necessarily reunion.

I mention this encounter because, if at all possible, speak to your offender no matter what you think the result might be. If it goes well, you won back a friend. If it goes poorly, you can take pride in being a "hero" because you took action. You didn't sit back like a coward and avoid the hard thing.

Having the conversation is so important I'm going to take two chapters to address it. The first chapter is about the spirit of the conversation while the second chapter is about the "how to" of the conversation.

Becoming A Peacemaker

Once, while teaching the steps to forgiveness, I mentioned the importance of speaking to one's offender. One well-churched person looked stunned and said, "You don't mean we are supposed to talk to our offender, right?" He honestly thought he misheard me. I said, "That's exactly what I mean. Jesus told us to seek out our offender and try to bring about reconciliation."

This is what I was referring to:
> If you are offering your gift at the altar and there remember that your brother or sister has something against you, leave your gift there in front of the altar. First **go and be reconciled to that person**; then come and offer your gift. Matthew 5:23,24 (emphasis added)

The reason Jesus tells us to "go and be reconciled" is because there is nothing more important to God than restoring broken relationships. To the religious person he says it's even more important than "worship" (presenting an offering at the altar).

When you follow God, stories of forgiveness and reconciliation should follow you in your wake. If you lack these stories, you might not be the spiritual person you think you are.

There are many great stories about Cedarbrook Church, the church where I pastor. There's the story of how we started with twenty people. There's the story of how we raised over a million dollars...twice...to build and pay off a church building. There's the story of our growth and the many people we've been able to help locally, nationally, and internationally. I'm grateful for these stories, but if we don't have stories of broken relationships being restored, then we have a problem. There is a big disconnect that needs to be addressed.

God is a god of reconciliation. The Cedarbrook community should be known as people who forgive and reconcile much more than people who raise money, erect buildings, or have an "awesome" band. Does God really care that much about these things in comparison to his followers exhibiting humility, compassion, and forgiveness? I don't think he does.

Some church people don't believe talking about restoring

relationships is the "gospel," that is, the main Bible message. They might concede it's biblical, but it's not the core message. They believe the gospel is the story of God and how he came to save us. Sermons should be about God and not relationships.

I can't disagree more. The story of God saving us is only half of our message. The other half of our message is how God saving us plays out in our lives day to day. If we connect with God but struggle connecting with others, then something is wrong with that picture.

Reconciliation. Forgiveness. Unity. These are not marginal issues of faith. They are central.

Steps To Making Peace

In an earlier chapter I said we do a number of things to cause broken relationships. I mentioned seven things that tick us off: invalidation, exposed weaknesses, trauma, limited choices, embarrassing behavior, irritating behavior, and unmet needs. The first two in this list have something in common. They both involve *speaking*. Our words have an incredible ability to hurt people. A few poorly chosen words can cause a relationship to stall, sputter, and spiral out of control. If there isn't some kind of intervention, the relationship can actually crash and burn. Maybe you've experienced that.

Have you ever heard these words?

> *I can't believe what he said to me.*
>
> *Why would she say that? It hurt so much.*
>
> *Their words cut like a knife.*
>
> *They made me feel like a fool. I felt so small.*
>
> *I can't get their words out of my mind. I'll never forget what they said.*

There is a letter in the Bible written to a church full of broken relationships. We don't know exactly what was going on, but they were going through some kind of trial. Instead of pulling together to face their trial, there were all kinds of infighting. This is what the author says to them:

> What causes fights and quarrels among you? Don't they come from your desires that battle within you? You desire but do not have, so you kill. You covet but you cannot get what you want, so you quarrel and fight. James 4:1,2

James is not happy with them. He doesn't mince words. Throughout his letter he tells them exactly what they need to do to restore their relationships. They need to be peacemakers. Peacemakers are intentional about restoring broken relationships. Following is some of his instruction to them:

1. Be Slow To Speak

The first thing James tells them is peacemakers listen well and are slow to respond.

> Everyone should be quick to listen, slow to speak and slow to become angry, because our anger does not produce the righteousness that God desires. James 1:19,20

Someone pointed out to me the word LISTEN has the same letters as the word SILENT. (And no...it wasn't my wife!) If you want to truly listen to someone, first be quiet. When the other person pauses, it's not your opportunity to jump in with your story, but rather, ask a question, like: *What do mean by that?* You want to draw them out. Ask them to tell you more, or ask: *Can you give me an example? How do you feel about that?*

I admit I'm not always good at this. Solutions come quickly to me. I want to move on, not sit around and talk about "feelings" or the nuances of the disagreement. I'm action oriented, but when I am quick to act, I am also quick to offend.

Listening and asking questions does the opposite. They tell the other person, *You matter to me*, and *I care about you*. That's important if you want to restore a relationship.

We've all been on the other end of people *not* listening. We know what it's like not feeling heard or understood. It's alienating, that is, it makes you feel like an *alien:* different and alone. You feel odd and isolated. It can be very painful. When someone listens well that all changes: you feel understood, valued, and connected.

God made us to connect. Connection brings us our greatest joy, and disconnection brings us our greatest pain.

James gives us some insight into our tendency to shoot off our mouth in anger:

> ...our anger does not produce the righteousness that God desires. James 1:20

In other words: just getting mad at someone, telling them off, or telling them what they should do doesn't work. It doesn't fix anything. Have you ever noticed that? When's the last time telling someone off really solved the problem and brought unity? James says...*never*. It never happens. If the method you use to solve problems isn't working, pick a different method.

Here's your new method; *be quick to listen, slow to speak, and slow to anger.*

2. Tame Your Tongue

The second thing James tells us is peacemakers watch their words.

> Those who consider themselves religious and yet do not keep a tight rein on their tongues deceive themselves, and their religion is worthless. James 1:26

That's pretty strong. He says your faith is *meaningless*...it's a farce, if you can't control your words. So let me ask you...do you have a tight rein on your tongue?

Speaking of "a tight rein" is a horse metaphor. About halfway through his letter James brings this up again and adds a second metaphor: that of a ship.

> Those who are never at fault in what they say are perfect, able to keep their whole body in check. When we put bits into the mouths of horses to make them obey us, we can turn the whole animal. Or take ships as an example. Although they are so large and are driven by strong winds, they are steered by a very small rudder wherever the pilot wants to go. James 3:2-4

His point is: if you control your mouth, you are a powerful person. You are able to use the energy of your anger to be constructive, not destructive. If you don't have control of your mouth you can cause all kinds of problems.

> Consider what a great forest is set on fire by a small spark. The tongue also is a fire, a world of evil among the parts of the body. It corrupts the whole person, sets the whole course of one's life on fire, and is itself set on fire by hell. James 4:5,6

Again, he uses strong language here, almost over the top. Look at the words he chooses: *fire, evil, corrupts, hell.* He tells them that their inability to handle their anger appropriately turns them into a tool of the devil. He purposefully shocks them to get their attention.

Too often, rather than controlling our anger, we just do what feels good. What feels good in the moment is to blow up. We let someone have it.

James continues:

> With the tongue we praise our Lord and Father, and with it we curse human beings, who have been made in God's likeness. Out of the same mouth come praise and cursing. My brothers and sisters, this should not be. James 3:9,10

If we care about somebody, if we care about a relationship...*this should not be*. If we consider ourselves children of God, we should speak in a way that preserves the dignity of the other person. We should never speak to people in a way that invalidates them or makes them feel they are less than we are. We'll never restore a broken relationship this way.

James offers an alternative. He talks about being a peacemaker. The last verse in this chapter says:

> Peacemakers who sow in peace reap a harvest of righteousness. James 3:18

Do you remember what James said in chapter one about how anger doesn't work the righteousness of God? This is his answer to what *does* work the righteousness of God. He says if you want to please God: plant peace, not anger. James says we plant peace with our words. It's like the book of Proverbs says:

> Some people make cutting remarks, but the words of the wise bring healing. Proverbs 12:18

3. Approach The Person With The Right Attitude

The third quality of a peacemaker is they are careful to approach the other person with the right attitude. James tells us how to do that.

> But the wisdom that comes from heaven is first of all **pure**; then **peace loving, considerate, submissive, full of mercy and good fruit, impartial** and **sincere.** Peacemakers who sow in peace reap a harvest of righteousness. James 3:17,18 (emphasis added)

I'm going to briefly look at each of these words and unpack them for you. What I want you to see is how each word describes an attitude that *builds trust*. Broken relationships are about broken trust. If you want to restore the relationship, trust must be rebuilt.

PURE. Pure means "untainted" or having "no mixed motive." When you talk to someone don't go to them with selfish intentions. Don't go to "get" something. You shouldn't have any agenda other than to connect: to hear them and understand them.

PEACE LOVING. This means you park any kind of anger or animosity at the door. You want to communicate to the other person you aren't coming for a fight. It's like when you enter someone's home you often kick off your shoes. Why? Because you don't want to track on their carpet. But it's also a sign of respect. You send out this little signal that says, "I respect you. I'm entering your personal space, and I'm letting you know that I'm not going to mess it up."

Occasionally you get someone in your house that doesn't do that. They just march right in and leave a trail of dirt behind them. You think, *Okay…this person is clueless. I need to watch them. I can't trust them to care for my house.* So you move them out of your space as quickly as possible.

It's the same way emotionally. It's important to send off signals that you "come in peace." You come to develop the relationship, not attack. We call a person like this "safe" which means we can trust them emotionally. It's like those old Western cowboy shows where they would meet with Native Americans to smoke a peace pipe. The ceremony was meant to communicate both sides intentions were peace loving.

CONSIDERATE. Other versions of the Bible translate this word as *gentle, fair,* and *appropriate.* On the flip side we know what it means to be "inappropriate." We think of someone who is blunt, abrasive, or insensitive.

Maybe kindness is a good word here. I've got a friend who has often quoted Plato to me:

> Be kind, for everyone you meet is fighting a hard battle.

I like that. What if you pretend that people you meet just had a big fight with a loved one, or got bad news from the doctor, or got laid off from their job? They probably aren't going to tell you about the battle they are fighting. But would you speak differently to them if you knew they were fighting a big battle? I bet you would; you'd be more considerate and cut them a lot of slack.

SUBMISSIVE. This word didn't make any sense to me at first. After doing a little study I decided it relates to what I said about listening. It means you are focused on the other person. They have your full attention. You are actively listening to them (submitting to listen to what they have to say) and working at seeing things from their perspective.

It's not easy. In fact, that's why we tend to be friends with people like us. We don't have to work very hard to understand them, but a peacemaker is willing to work at understanding even the people that are totally unlike them.

I recently spoke with a girl who is an atheist. She said she doesn't like to tell people she is an atheist because then they are often rude to her. They regularly tell her how wrong she is without bothering to listen to her (which I'm sure really compels her to believe in God). But a peacemaker would value what she has to say even if they disagreed with her.

FULL OF MERCY and **GOOD FRUIT**. These two words taken together mean you are willing to go beyond words and help the person you are talking to. Just a few verses earlier James says:

> Who is wise and understanding among you? Let them **show it by their good life, by deeds done** in the humility that comes from wisdom. James 3:13 (emphasis added)

That's what James means by being full of mercy and good fruit. When people see you are willing to take action, it builds their trust in you.

IMPARTIAL. This is an important word. It means to not discriminate against someone. Or a better way to say it is: *to not see the other person as different from you.*

This word is the essence of what it takes to restore broken relationships. The more I see you as different from me, the easier it is for me to separate myself from you. Isn't that right? It's the opposite of empathy. The farther apart I am from you, the easier it is for me to disrespect you. That's what happens with my new atheist friend. When people see her as "different," they feel much more comfortable berating her. If they took the time to see what they had in common with her, it would be harder to be rude to her because then they'd be mistreating "one of their own."

I read a story in Brene Brown's book, *I Thought It Was Just Me*, about a woman who was at a school event for her child. A very business-looking mom came up to her and asked her where she worked. The mom said, "I stay at home with my kids." As soon as she said this, the businesswoman lost interest in talking to her, walked away, and sought out other businesswomen. Rather than focus on what they had in common as moms, the businesswoman chose to focus on their differences. The experience caused the stay-at-home mom to feel alone and disconnected.

That's not how peacemakers think. Peacemakers look for what they share in common rather than how they are different. Commonalities bring us together. Differences alienate us. If you want to restore a relationship, dwell on what you share in common with the other person.

SINCERE. This word simply means to be genuine or real. Peacemakers don't just say something to keep you happy in the moment. They are the same person outside of the meeting as they are inside the meeting.

Peacemakers don't get stuck. They know how to keep their relationships clear of tension and drama. They are quick to listen. They control their words, and they know how to approach people with the right attitude to build trust.

Write it down:

- *Are you quick to listen or quick to speak? How has that helped or hurt you?*

- *Do your words bring healing or damage to troubled relationships? What can you do to promote healing with your words?*

- *Look at the eight characteristics of a peacemaker. Which do you do well? Which do you need to work on? Does your approach build trust or break trust?*

How to Confront Your Offender

I recently suggested to a friend that they needed to confront someone in their life. They sighed and said, "I could never do that." They went on to explain that whenever they try to confront someone they get so emotional they cry and end up apologizing for overreacting. It always backfires on them.

Of all the laments people have shared with me throughout the years, the one most repeated is, "I hate confronting people." That's too bad because an unwillingness to confront only means an inability to truly connect with people.

As much as we might find it uncomfortable, Jesus tells us to go to the person who has done something wrong.

> If your brother sins, **go and reprove him** in private; if he listens to you, you have won your brother. But if he does not listen to you, take one or two more with you, so that; by the mouth of two or three witnesses, every fact may be confirmed. And if he refuses to listen to them, tell it to the church; and if he refuses to listen even to the church, let him be to you as a Gentile and a tax-gatherer. Matthew 18:15-17 (emphasis added)

Let me make some observations about this passage that might help us to "have the conversation."

1. Confirm The Offense
Jesus starts by saying, "*If* your *brother* sins." There are two things to note here. First is the word "if." In other words, make sure there is a real offense before you go talk to the person. You don't want to make a big deal out of nothing. It might only strain your relationship.

2. Consider The Relationship
The other note in this phrase is the word "brother." The word "brother" implies a relationship – someone you know well. Jesus isn't giving you the right to be the moral police to confront every casual acquaintance you know about their behavior. A sit down confrontation should be about a significant offense with someone you know fairly well.

3. Write Out Your Thoughts In Advance

It's helpful to write out and explore potential conversations, working them through until you are confident you aren't going to inflame the situation. Remember the goal of your anger is to *resolve*, not *retaliate*. It might be helpful to include a friend or counselor in this. Consider the following as you prepare:

- **Take responsibility.** If you share guilt in the relationship, make sure you mention that first, and ask for their forgiveness. Your honesty and humility will set the tone for the meeting and enable them to humble themselves as well.
- **Seek a win-win.** Jesus said that the point of going to the person in private is to win them over, not condemn them.

This should be a *positive* encounter, so be very careful how you talk. The Bible tells us to make sure we tell people "the truth *in love*" (Ephesians 4:15). Our words should be spoken with the intent of building each other up, not tearing each other down.

> *Do not let any unwholesome talk come out of your mouths, but only what is helpful for building others up according to their needs, that it may benefit those who listen. And do not grieve the Holy Spirit of God, with whom you were sealed for the day of redemption. Get rid of all bitterness, rage and anger, brawling and slander, along with every form of malice. Be kind and compassionate to one another, forgiving each other, just as in Christ God forgave you. Ephesians 4:29-32*

- **Be safe.** The person you meet with will probably be nervous and defensive. Make sure you make statements that are non-threatening, open-ended, and allow for discussion. Here are two examples for you (neither reflects a true conversation, but they are helpful to make my point.) First the bad:

> *Thanks for meeting with me, Bob. I asked to meet with you because I want to let you know how much you hurt me the other day when you attacked me in front of our co-workers. You made me feel stupid, and it really ticked me off, but I want you to know that I forgive you.*

What's wrong with this picture? First, it is too abrupt. It gets right to the problem. Then it quickly turns into an accusation. It says, "You hurt me" and "You attacked me" making Bob sound like the aggressor. He may have been, but you don't want to paint him in a negative light if you want him to stay open to dialogue with you. Also, saying, "I want you to know I forgive you" sounds condescending, like it's obvious how terrible he was, and he can't wait to be forgiven by you. You want to make sure he knows he did something wrong before you say something like that.

Here's an improved version:
> *Thanks for meeting with me Bob. I want to speak with you about the meeting the other day at work. Do you remember when you said those things about my proposal in front of the team? Well, I'm sure you didn't mean any harm, but to be honest, I was offended. I felt like you were trying to make me look bad in front of the others. I'm sure that's not true, but that's how it felt, and I was embarrassed. I felt really stupid. I'd like to clear this up so it doesn't hurt our relationship. Can you help me understand what you were saying?*

Do you hear the difference? The first example is condescending and accusatory. The second example is simply a statement of how you felt and leaves the door open for Bob to explain himself. It also starts by making sure he remembers what happened instead of assuming he remembers. The first example focused on what Bob *did wrong*. That will only make Bob defensive. The second example focused on *how you felt*. That helps Bob to understand you better.

4. Correct In Private

Now that you have a script of what you want to say, look for the right place for the conversation. Never talk about someone's faults in front of another person. They will only feel shamed, and they might possibly shut down emotionally. Now, *you've* offended *them,* and the problem just got bigger. Pull them aside to speak about your concern, or set up a special time to meet you alone. That way they will know you are considerate of their feelings.

5. Choose A Good Place
A public place works well, like a restaurant, so the conversation can't get out of hand. If you choose a restaurant, make sure it's one where you can get some separation from other tables. You don't want your conversation to be overheard.

6. Read What You Wrote
If you are concerned about saying the wrong thing, or fear getting too emotional at your meeting, read from your script. It might seem a little awkward, but it will give you confidence that you will say the right thing. It will also assure the other party that you have thought this through and will not fly off the handle. Don't sit down and read a four-page letter. That's overwhelming. Write out statements and responses that you can refer to when appropriate. Give plenty of opportunity for the other person to respond to what you've said.

By reading your concerns you won't deviate from the purpose of your meeting. It might also be helpful to leave a copy of the script with your offender to make sure they have an accurate record of what was said.

7. Bring A Mutual Friend To Mediate
If you are concerned the situation might get ugly, or you won't make it emotionally without some support, then consider bringing a friend for support. Before you do that, get permission from your offender. They might feel threatened with a third party and shut down. It's best if you suggest a third party you both know and trust.

I hope you see the wisdom in going to your offender directly. Too often we "solve" our differences by *avoiding* our offender. That only leads to more misunderstanding which in turn slowly moves you farther and farther apart. Speaking to the person directly clears up misunderstandings and reopens the communication lines.

You might object: *What if they don't want to meet? What if they just blow me off?* That's *their* issue, not yours. You can't let the fear of their response dictate your behavior. Jesus told us the way to go. He wants us to speak with them and try to win them over. If they reject you, Jesus gives us the next step.

8. Go Back With Two Or Three Mutual, Trust-Worthy Friends

The point here isn't to shame your offender but humbly tell them of your sincere concern. In the world of addiction recovery we call this an "intervention." Usually when people see it's not just one person who is challenging them, but a room full of their closest friends and family, they will be more open to change.

9. If Necessary, Discontinue The Relationship

Jesus is a realist. He understands that some people will continue to reject you. There may come a time when you need to communicate to others what has happened and discontinue the relationship. (By the way, this is another biblical example of setting boundaries.) Reconciliation has failed, but at least you tried. You made the attempt. Like Paul said in the book of Romans:

> Do not repay anyone evil for evil. Be careful to do what is right in the eyes of everybody. If it is possible, **as far as it depends on you, live at peace with everyone.** Romans 12:17,18 (emphasis added)

Do you remember the former partner I met with unsuccessfully? He died a few years later unexpectedly. What a shock. I was so sad that we never reconnected, but at least I know I tried rather than let the rift go untreated. Could I have done more? Probably. I know so much more about reconciliation now than I did then. But I did the best I could with the knowledge I had at the time.

Lewis Smedes put it well when he said:

> The climax of forgiveness takes two, I know. But you can have the reality of forgiving without its climax. You do not always need a thing whole to enjoy it all. A blossom has real beauty even if it never becomes a flower. A climb can be successful though we do not reach the summit. Forgiving is real even if

it stops at the healing of the forgiver.[56]

Final Thoughts

You might question if the meeting has to be in person. If at all possible, yes. Meeting via phone, email, or letter always leaves too much to the imagination. You can't see the body language or hear the tone of the voice (with an email or letter). Plus, you are less likely to clarify any confusion. Do what you can to meet in person. Of course, if you think it might get hostile, then a letter might actually be the best way to go.

People often ask me: *What if the person who offended you is dead? What if they don't want to speak to you? What if speaking to the other person isn't appropriate? Is forgiveness thwarted?* Not at all. You are the one who forgives. You are the one who gives up the right to get even. You don't need the other person in your presence, or to do anything, to achieve forgiveness. I recommend going to the other person because Jesus told us to, but also because it brings clarity and closure. But forgiveness can still be achieved without seeing your offender.

Write it down:

- *Who is it you need to talk to? Make it a priority.* Before you go any further in this study, make plans to contact the person or people who have offended you.

---

[56] *Forgive and Forget*, p. 70

Chapter Nineteen:

When Nothing Works

Not long ago, I taught a series at my church about how to restore broken relationships. A friend of mine came up to me halfway through the series and said, "You know, this doesn't always work. Relationships can't always be reconciled."

He knew what he was talking about. He had been working to draw closer to his family for the past few years, and it wasn't working.

I agreed. *That's reality*. Broken relationships can't always be resolved the way we would like. So I asked my friend to share his story to close out the series. His name is Byron. Let me recap Byron's talk for you.

In the early days, Byron's siblings connected to each other in three ways: through their parents, the family farm, and their church. They were one big happy family and assumed they always would be. But as the siblings grew up and moved away, they no longer had the farm or church to hold them together. Thankfully holidays with mom and dad, and fond memories, still kept them close.

As the health of Byron's aging parents started to fail, his siblings drew even closer as they shared the same purpose of helping them. But when mom and dad passed away things changed. The siblings no longer had time for each other. Byron related how he sensed a profound loss: not only were his parents gone but the sense of "family."

Byron didn't want to be passive about this loss, so he created opportunities for his siblings to come together. But most chose to ignore these opportunities. The family that was once seemingly so close was now distant.

This was disillusioning to Byron. *How could this happen? Aren't we family? Aren't we all Christians?* After reflecting on these questions he realized how the three things that kept his siblings together no longer existed: his parents, the farm, and their common church experience. Without these factors they were little more than acquaintances.

Byron slowly came to understand that he needed to accept this "new normal," grieve it, and come up with a plan of action. He developed personal rules of engagement: a plan for how he would communicate with his siblings without putting pressure on them to respond. I offer them to you here (with my commentary) because our congregation found them very helpful. Maybe it will help you as well.

Family Rules of Engagement:[57]

- **I will extend courtesy, keep an open mind, and be kind.** Byron doesn't want to withhold kindness out of spite. Who knows? Maybe there is still hope.
- **I will expect nothing but also close nothing. I will burn no bridges.** This is a hard balance to keep. He doesn't want to get his hopes up only to be disappointed, but he also doesn't want to miss an opportunity to connect should it present itself.
- **I will participate when invited** (i.e. weddings, graduations). He doesn't want to give anyone the cold shoulder or imply that he's not interested in the family.
- **I will send birthday and Christmas cards with no strings attached:** *simple, kind, and caring.* He refuses to include subtle messages of how much he'd like to get together or spread guilt for family members not joining him.
- **I will call if I have a tragedy with no guilt implied.** He will contact his family as a courtesy, but he doesn't expect them to drop everything and come.
- **I will pray about my attitude and theirs.** This will help guard their hearts from closing off from each other.
- **I will respect their desire for privacy or space.** Just because they are family doesn't mean they have to be together. He will work at dropping that expectation of people.
- **Things can change, they can change, and I can change.** Byron recognizes that this feeling of distance may be just a season. Some day they may be close again.

Many of us never gain the insight into our family that Bryon has. We live confused and depressed that we are not close as a family. We nag, manipulate, and guilt our families to be what we want them to be, but that only makes things worse.

Byron has done a good job of dealing with the offense of his family. He

---

[57] Adapted from the sermon series, *Restoring Broken Relationships*, with Byron Anderson, July 1, 2012, Cedarbrook Church. Visit cedarbrookchurch.net/sermons to listen to the full message.

has chosen to not get even, eliminated expectations, reframed his situation, and kept an open mind about the future. You may want to adopt these same rules of engagement for your own family.

Chapter Twenty:

Forgiveness and Beyond

Forgiveness has many layers to it. In some ways, it's a never-ending process, often a daily discipline that you apply throughout your day to different people and situations. Here are a few more ideas to make sure that once you get unstuck, you stay unstuck.

1. Transfer The Ownership
This idea came from another pastor. When you sell your car to another person, you sign over the title. This pastor prints up an actual title of ownership. He has his client write out the details of their offense, just like a car title has the details on the make and the model of the car. Then he has the person sign over the title. He dates it and stamps GOD at the bottom as the new owner of the offense. Either he keeps the title or lets the people burn the title: symbolizing the offense is no longer theirs to own.

Whether you use this exercise or not, the concept is what needs to happen in your mind for forgiveness to take place. Forgiveness means transferring the ownership of the offense to God. It means letting go...for good. If you are a visual person, this exercise might make forgiveness real to you.

2. Maintain Your Forgiveness

If you've been able to forgive your offender as a result of this book and get on with your life, I'm thrilled. Before you think you've arrived, there is the issue of *maintaining* forgiveness. Forgiveness is a process more than an event. As much as I'd like to tell you that, once you forgive, your problems are over, that's just not true.

Do you remember the story I told about Chip and Jody Ferlaak? Oprah Winfrey asked Jody if she had to work at forgiveness every day. Jody replied:
> Every day. I feel I fight to make that choice to forgive because I wake up and I don't feel like I want to forgive this woman. You know, you wake up and you realize that the nightmare is still there: Teagan's not there (her daughter who died in the car crash). It actually happened. So it's a conscious choice.

Jody said it was work to forgive. It requires routine maintenance: a continual choosing.

But remember: God is there just as much on the one thousandth day as he was on the first day to help you forgive. Over time, you'll need less and less help as forgiveness takes effect. It's often three steps forward and two steps back, but over time it's still progress.

John Trent describes it by saying:
> Most of us forgive in steps. Instead of making one sweeping judicial pardon, we usually forgive specifics as they come to our minds. That's why it's important to keep that picture before us. It helps us to grow in our understanding as new pieces of information may cause us to see the picture differently. And as we grow in our understanding, we will grow in our capacity to feel compassion, which will lead us

into fuller expressions of forgiveness.[58]

3. Bless Your Offender

The thought of forgiving your offender might be a tremendous challenge. You might wonder how that can even happen, but believe it or not, there is a place that goes beyond forgiveness. It's when you are able to *bless* your offender. To forgive and to bless are closely related, but they are definitely different.

To forgive means to *not* give your offender what they deserve: justice. To bless means to *give* your offender a gift they *do not* deserve: kindness. Jesus said:
> I tell you …Love your enemies, do good to those who hate you, bless those who curse you, pray for those who mistreat you. If someone strikes you on one cheek, turn to him the other also. If someone takes your cloak, do not stop him from taking your tunic. Give to everyone who asks you, and if anyone takes what belongs to you, do not demand it back. Do to others as you would have them do to you. Luke 6:28-31

When I talk about blessing your offender, I'm not talking about being phony or giving them gifts. I'm talking about offering them simple kindness: including them in conversation, choosing to not withhold small favors, speaking well of them, or choosing to not speak poorly of them.

Here is a simple example. A few years ago I had a run-in with a leader of my former church denomination. Our church had recently joined the denomination. We met for lunch and one of the first things this leader wanted to make clear to me was that he wanted our church to give financial support to the denomination. I was taken aback and told him so. I had just met him, and our church was new to the denomination. Did he really think that talking to me about money was the best way to start our relationship? I told him how disappointed I was in his approach, and we left on icy terms. (I hadn't developed my

---

[58] *Choosing to Live the Blessing*, p.77

peacemaking skills at that time!)

Later on this person was nominated for an executive position in the denomination. It was tempting to vote against him after he had treated me the way he did. But I realized that I shouldn't label the man as a bad person just because of one bad experience with him. I chose to bless him instead and gave him my vote.

If you struggle with forgiveness, then *blessing* may be mind bending. But I want you to keep the idea of blessing in your mind. It's an important part of the forgiveness discussion.

Who Benefits From Forgiveness?

As I've read about forgiveness in our culture I've noticed a definite shift away from forgiveness being for the offender to forgiveness being exclusively for the victim. I agree with this to some extent. It was the focus of much of this book, but to stop at the self-serving aspects of forgiveness is to miss the full idea and spiritual implications of forgiveness. I'm concerned with the attitude that says: *If forgiveness helps me move on with my life then great, I'm all for it. If it only helps my offender then I'm not interested.*

I appreciate the writing of Miroslav Volf because he holds forgiveness to the highest level. He understands we forgive others as a way of reflecting our gratitude for how God forgives us. In his book, *Free of Charge*, he says:

>...we should give primarily for others sake not our own.[59]

>We should absorb the wrongdoing in order to transform the wrongdoers.[60]

This kind of attitude isn't rooted in selfishness but in the love of God and the kingdom of God.

You might want to forgive to simply break free from your offender. You might not have any aspirations beyond that. That's a good start and a

---

[59] *Free of Charge*, p. 168
[60] Ibid, p. 161

huge step forward. But if you are interested in the full depths of forgiveness and following Jesus to the utmost, I hope you will consider taking your forgiveness to a higher level. But let's not forget that forgiveness can also release a wrongdoer from judgment and free them to change. This is what Volf refers to when he says that forgiveness "absorbs the wrongdoing." If everyone condemns me it is very hard for me to change. But if my community forgives me, and gives me opportunities to start over, I may be inspired to change: to become a new person.

This is what Jesus offers *us*. If at all possible, this is what we can offer *others*.

If you can forgive your offender, you will not only free yourself from being stuck, you may free your offender as well.

Write it down:
- Consider transferring the ownership of your anger to God. Imagine that happening. *How does it feel to know that you no longer have to take responsibility to maintain your anger?*

- *What will it require to continually maintain your forgiveness?*

- *Do you think it is possible for you to ever take your forgiveness to the point of blessing your offender? What would need to happen for that to take place?*

Blessing Your Offender

Nothing reveals the *reality* of God better than a wounded person *forgiving* her offender.

Nothing reveals the *glory* of God better than a wounded person *blessing* her offender.

I want to share a story of blessing with you. It's about a man by the name of Walt Everett.[61] He was able to both forgive and bless.

Back in the late 1980's, Walt's son was shot in cold blood as he entered his apartment. The man who pulled the trigger lived across the hall and was strung out on cocaine.

At first, Walt was filled with rage and contempt for his son's murderer, whose name was Mike. Walt's anger dominated his life. At the trial Mike was contrite and apologetic. With a broken spirit he told the court how sorry he was.

Over the months that passed, God enabled Walt to forgive Mike. One night he sat down and wrote Mike a letter. Walt tells about it like this:
> I told Mike of the anger and the bewilderment, the frustration, the wondering how anyone could think he had the right to determine when anybody else should stop living. I went through about a page-and-a-half of that, and finally I wrote, "Having said all of that, I want to thank you for saying you were sorry in court, and as hard as these words are to write, I forgive you."[62]

That's powerful, but the story doesn't end there. After receiving the letter, Mike was so moved by Walt's forgiveness that he turned his life over to God. Then he invited Walt to visit him in prison. Walt said he was shocked at the request. He thought after he sent his letter to Mike he could put it all in the past and move on. He never considered meeting his son's killer face to face. He wasn't sure if he should do it.

He wasn't sure if he *could* do it, but he felt it was something God wanted him to do.

Finally, the day came when they met. After the two of them had talked for some time, Walt describes what happened:
> When I got up to leave, we started shaking hands, and we instinctively embraced. I guess God was making the motion,

---

[61] Paul Solotaroff, *Forgiving the Murderer*, (Rolling Stone), June 24, 2004
[62] *New Man Magazine*, 1998

because both of us moved at the same time. We both broke down in tears.

After that moment, Walt's life was never the same.

Walt saw a genuine change in Mike's life. He decided to seek Mike's parole, releasing him from prison after only four years behind bars. To everyone's surprise, the parole was granted. When Mike got married, Walt participated in his wedding. Since then the two have remained friends, even speaking together at churches, telling their story.

Not everyone was happy with Walt's new friend. Walt said:
> Somebody said to me, "I can understand forgiving him, but do you have to be friends with him?" Then I said, "I thought there was something about being friends involved in forgiveness. Jesus calls us to forgive – I thought that meant that, when it's possible, you are to have a relationship with that person."

Walt understood something about God's forgiveness few of us do. Walt didn't stop at sending a letter to proclaim his forgiveness. He took the big risk and entered into Mike's life. He entered his prison, spoke to him, and understood him. He embraced him, sought his parole, and became Mike's friend, even though Mike didn't deserve any of it.

Walt went beyond forgiving. He chose to bless as well. This is why I believe that blessing reveals the glory of God. It is something *supernatural*.

This is a shocking story. It's illogical; it doesn't make any sense to the natural mind. To some this story is even repulsive as they imagine embracing their child's killer. I haven't told this story yet without someone saying, "He's crazy. I'd never do that."

But God only gives us what we need when we need it. He doesn't give us the ability to forgive or bless until the time is right.

You *can* forgive. You *can* bless, with God's help.

Welsh poet and priest, George Herbert, said:
> Forgiveness is the fragrance of the violet, which still clings fast to the heel that crushed it.

That's a beautiful picture of the power of forgiveness to transform an offense. Do you believe God can give you the perfume necessary for this: that even after a deep wound you reflect the humility and goodness of God?

My prayer for you is that each time you are crushed you will give off the sweet fragrance of forgiveness rather than the stench of bitterness. When you forgive it shows your heart has opened to receive the goodness of God: not only for you but for the person you forgave.

Wouldn't it be amazing if the offense that almost kept you stuck, led you, and your offender, to a place of personal transformation?

Write it down:

- *What troubles you the most about Walt's story?*

- *Is there anything in his story that resonates with you?*

- *As you consider forgiveness would you say your desire is simply to help yourself, or is there anything in you that hopes your forgiveness might bless your offender?*

- *Do you think God could transform you to the point that, when crushed, you gave off a sweet fragrance?*

Part Four

The Other Side of Forgiveness

Most of this book focuses on how to forgive others so you can move on with your life. But sometimes you get stuck because others can't forgive you, or you can't forgive yourself. In the closing chapters, I want to address the other side of forgiveness.

Chapter Twenty-One

How to Be Reconciled

When Scott hit forty he realized that a "midlife crisis" was not a myth. It was a reality. He assumed that, at his age, he would have achieved more significance. He thought he'd be farther in his career, a better father, and more in love with his wife. None of these were true.

He didn't go looking for an affair, but he was certainly primed for one.

Scott traveled twice a month with a crew from work: one of them being Julie, a recently divorced account executive. She caught his eye whenever she entered the room. He had to admit he enjoyed being in her presence and found himself adjusting his schedule to be where she would be.

One night Scott and his co-workers finished off the day in the hotel bar. As everyone signed off for the night, he and Julie ended up being the last ones sitting at the table. They enjoyed one last drink together and took the same elevator up to the same floor. As Scott paused momentarily before entering his room, Julie paused long enough to show that she was interested in joining him. Whether it was the three drinks, his mid-life issues, or general fatigue, he chose to welcome her in and begin a two-year affair.

Without going into the details, it all ended poorly. (Does it ever end well?) His wife was devastated, his children were disillusioned, and Scott was even unhappier than before. His wife seriously considered divorce, which Scott didn't want. He wanted forgiveness, but no matter what he said or did it seemed he only made things worse.

An Effective Apology

Many people like Scott want forgiveness but fail to find it. They either don't know what to do, or they do the *right* things *poorly*. In this chapter I will give you some practical steps to help you restore a relationship that your behavior has broken.

I called this chapter *How to Be Reconciled* because Jesus said:
> ...if you are offering your gift at the altar and there remember that your brother has something against you, leave your gift there in front of the altar. **First go and be reconciled** to your brother; then come and offer your gift. Matthew 5:23 (emphasis added)

I referred to this text earlier. When Jesus first started talking about bringing a gift to the altar, I bet his disciples' ears perked up. They leaned forward to hear some inside information on what would really impress God during the offering of their sacrifice. What prayer could they recite, or what ritual could they perform, to catch God's attention? Instead, Jesus surprised them by talking about reconciliation! He said:

> *If you've done something to offend another person, then forget the sacrifice. It's meaningless. The most worshipful thing you can do isn't going to church – or singing louder – or putting more money in the offering. The most worshipful thing you can do is to go and be reconciled to the person you've offended.*

Jesus didn't tell them to go and make excuses for their behavior. He didn't tell them to go and say, "I'm sorry." His goal was much higher. He said, "Go and be *reconciled*." The word "reconciled" means to create an entirely new relationship. It doesn't mean to simply patch it back together and move on. It implies a rebirth of the relationship.

When it comes to reconciliation, we often let ourselves off the hook too easily. We go, make a weak apology, and then pat ourselves on the back thinking we obeyed Jesus. But we didn't. If we weren't reconciled (or at least made the attempt), if the relationship wasn't transformed and brought to a new level of intimacy, then we didn't do what Jesus told us to do.

Jesus looks for results. We often look for a process. Jesus says *I don't care how you do it* (that is, the process you use), *just be reconciled* (the result). We say, *The cost of reconciliation scares me. I just want to do the least amount by way of apologizing and then move on.* As is so often the case, we differ with the ways of God because God seeks to build *relationship* while we are often content to simply obey *rules*.

The Offender's Role In Forgiveness

Too often, the responsibility of forgiveness lands on the victim. They feel it is their responsibility to mend the relationship. But the offender can facilitate their forgiveness and speed the reconciliation process with an effective apology.

Let me frame this in a personal way. Imagine I significantly betrayed you. Imagine you are hurt and question whether or not you want to still be my friend. What is it you need from me to help you forgive and restore our friendship? There are four things you most likely want from me.

1. Admit The Offense

Quite frankly, there is a lot in me working against admitting I'm wrong. Admitting my failure makes me feel bad. It makes me feel stupid. It makes me feel weak, so I'm not very motivated to admit anything.

At the same time I know I can't ignore what's obvious to you and everyone else, so my brain automatically comes up with a number of "solutions" to solve this tension. They give me a way to "admit" without really exposing any wrongdoing on my part. One solution is to **minimize** what I've done wrong. I make it sound like it isn't really as bad as you think it is. It's no big deal.

The second thing I might do is **blame** others. I blame people. I blame my car. I blame the weather. I blame the way my parents raised me. I blame my church. I might even blame you to put you on the defensive. I might say, "I was wrong, but so were you." I spread the blame far and wide to divert your attention away from my failure.

The third thing I might do is **rationalize** my offense: come up with great excuses for what I did. I mean, if you only knew my circumstances, the stress I'm under, my trouble at home, the financial hardship I'm dealing with, you'd see that what I did was totally acceptable. You would do the same.

If I do a good job of minimizing, blaming, and rationalizing, by the time I'm done, you'll feel sorry for me. You might even feel guilty for ever being mad. The problem with these tactics is they can make a bad situation worse because you aren't looking for excuses. You want honesty. You want the truth, the *whole* truth. You want full disclosure. You want to see I'm in touch with reality, and I have both the humility and the courage to admit what I've done wrong. If I don't give you this level of honesty then you might end up getting even madder.

The interesting thing here is that what you want is the opposite of what I feel is good for me. I *feel* like the more I admit, the less you'll like me, and the less of a chance we'll get back together. That's why I work so hard at a cover up.

The truth is: the more I admit, the greater the chance we have at reconciliation. Most people can handle the truth if it's *all* the truth. What they can't handle is deception because it soils the relationship. It creates distrust and suspicion, which only undermine the relationship.

There's something cleansing about the truth being told: for the teller and hearer. When you tell the truth it often creates trust, which is foundational to reconciliation. Yes, the truth might destroy the relationship, but so will withholding the truth. Withholding the truth might keep you in a relationship, but it will be based on a lie. It will be superficial. If the truth ever comes out (which it usually does), your friend or loved one will lose even more respect for you.

2. Express Sorrow

After I fully admit what I've done, what do you want to hear from me next? I think you want me to show remorse. You want to know I feel bad about what I did, and I understand how it impacted you.

Sorrow isn't just saying, "I'm sorry." Parents make this mistake. When Bobby throws mud in his sister's face, what do we tell Bobby? "Bobby, go tell your sister you are sorry." Bobby says, "I'm sorry" and then sticks his tongue out at her. That's not what I'm talking about.

Or has this ever happened? You have an argument where someone is trying to get you to apologize, and finally out of frustration you say, "*Okay, FINE! I'm SORRY! There, are you happy now?*" That's not sorrow either.

We see people make poor apologies in the media all the time, typically athletes and politicians. They'll do something stupid and then call a press conference and say:

> *I'd like to offer an apology for* (insert stupid thing here). *I understand some people are upset I did this. It was never my intention to offend anyone, but if anyone was offended then I'm sorry.*

Isn't that what they always say? It's like there is an apology script you can download off the internet because they all say the same thing.

What's wrong with that apology? There is no admission of guilt. The dictionary defines an apology as an "admission of guilt accompanied by regret."

Have you ever gotten a non-apology like that? What did it do for your relationship with your apologizer? It probably made it worse. Or what about you? Have you ever *offered* a non-apology like that? Oops. Yeah, we've all done it.

This kind of apology says the offender is sorry people got mad. It's like saying, "If you are so foolish to be mad about what I did, then I'm sorry for you," but they don't have any sense of doing wrong. They aren't sorry for what they did. They only apologized because their agent told them to apologize.

Sorrow Is Not About Me

The key to my expressing sorrow for offending you is expressing it in *your* terms. If you think about it, there are many reasons I might be sorry that have nothing to do with your pain. I might be sorry I got caught, sorry for the consequences, sorry it made me look bad, sorry others are mad, or sorry you think less of me. But if I'm not sorry for the hurt I've caused you, then it's not the sorrow you are looking for.

The kind of sorrow you want to hear from me is that I feel *your* pain; I understand how *you* must feel. You want to know I spent time thinking about how I hurt you and how you feel about it. That's called **empathy**. My apology needs to be rooted in *your* feelings. I should carefully choose words that convey to you I understand the impact of my actions. For example, it would help to say something like this:

> *I've been thinking about what I did and how it impacted you. If someone did to me what I did to you, I'd feel disrespected and abandoned. I'd feel taken for granted, and I'd want to shut them out of my life. I just want you to know I appreciate any hard feelings you might have toward me. They are totally justified.*

Notice I didn't tell you how you feel. No one likes to be told how he or she feels because I don't really know how you feel. What I said was, *this is how I would feel if I were in your shoes.* If what I say matches how you feel, then your trust for me grows. You might say to yourself, *Amazing.*

He actually gets it. I finally feel understood. Maybe there is hope after all. If what I said didn't match your feelings then I should invite you to tell me exactly how you do, in fact, feel.

Husbands and wives around the world are at an impasse in their relationship because of this very issue. They are sorry for their actions but are clueless as to how they wounded the other emotionally. Instead of reconciling, they only add insult to injury because they fail to recognize the true nature of the offense. They think they have "done their job" by saying they are sorry, when in reality, they failed to see the deeper issue dividing them.

For example, I might apologize to my wife for coming home late on a regular basis, but it's more than being late to her. She feels like I don't value time with the family. She feels disrespected and devalued (secondary losses). Until I realize the deeper issues and communicate my regret in terms she can relate to, my asking forgiveness is shallow to her, maybe even offensive. The apology ends up doing more harm than good.

3. Ask To Be Forgiven

So far, I've admitted my offense and expressed true sorrow. Is that enough? Are we good? Not quite. My apology needs something else: to ask to be forgiven.

I wonder how many times in your life someone has looked you in the eyes, admitted they were wrong (with no excuses), told you they were truly sorry, asked you to forgive them, and then sat waiting for your response. I bet you can count the number of times on one hand. Or how many times have you done that? We aren't very good at this.

When we apologize, we like to assume there is an implied request for forgiveness. This makes it easier on us, but I believe it's important to explicitly ask to be forgiven, especially with the bigger offenses. Look the person in the eye and ask, "Will you forgive me?" and then be quiet. Don't dilute the question by rattling on for five minutes. Just ask the question, and wait for their response.

Most of us don't do this. We might say, "I'm sorry." Or we might add, "I hope you can forgive me" and assume forgiveness will be granted. Sometimes people let us off the hook and say, "I forgive you." That's always nice because they offered it without us having to ask for it. Often they simply nod and say nothing. The question of forgiveness hangs in the air unanswered. We never really know if they forgave us or not. That's not good. We need to ask the question and the offended needs to answer it so we can have closure. We should know the status of the relationship. No one should assume anything.

Humility Helps

Do you know why it's so hard to ask for forgiveness? It's too humbling. It's like kneeling before your friend and laying the relationship at their feet saying, "You have the power to let this relationship live or die. I messed up. I no longer have the power in the relationship. You do." That's hard to swallow.

In ancient times, kings had the "power of the sword." If you came into the presence of a king they had the right to kill you on the spot if they didn't like you. They had all the power in the relationship.

It's the same way when I ask your forgiveness. I give you all the power. Unfortunately, most of us are too proud to humble ourselves to that extent. We aren't willing to give up the power so we hedge by simply saying, "I'm sorry." But humility is exactly what you want from me if I've offended you, isn't it? Although it is hard to ask for forgiveness, it is critical to the process of restoring a broken relationship.

Jesus is our ultimate example of humility. The Bible says:
> Your attitude should be the same as that of Christ Jesus: Who, being in very nature God, did not consider equality with God something to be grasped, but made himself nothing, taking the very nature of a servant, being made in human likeness. And being found in appearance as a man, he humbled himself and became obedient to death-- even death on a cross! Philippians 2:5-8

Asking to be forgiven requires a death: a death to all of your self-preserving justifications and rationalizations. It's a death to the perfect image that you try to project to people. But if you are willing to die, there is a good chance your relationship will be resurrected and transformed, which is the true meaning of reconciliation.

If you remember my discussion of "reframing the results" I said, in order to forgive, the *victim* needs to die to their expectations. Now we are looking at the other side of the equation. I'm asking the *offender* to die as well. If both parties can humble themselves through a "death" then forgiveness has a chance to exist.

Admitting the offense shows *honesty*. Expressing sorrow shows *empathy*. Asking forgiveness shows *humility*. Each of these is essential to reconciling a relationship. One more step remains.

4. Rebuild Trust

If I'm serious about restoring our broken relationship then it's important for me to rebuild your trust. It's great to have an apology, but you want to know if things are going to change. If I just keep repeating the offense over and over, my apology is empty. The Bible talks about a "godly sorrow" which means a sorrow that causes me to change my behavior (2 Corinthians 7:8-10). A change of behavior is the ultimate proof I am truly sorry for what I've done and sincere about restoring the relationship.

The sad reality is it takes years to build trust and only a second to break it. When that happens you have to take action to win back trust.

It's like you were standing with your friend, but when the offense occurred: the ground shifted, a valley opened up between the two of you, and now your are far apart. If you want to get back together, it's up to you to build a bridge back to them. The greater the gulf, the larger and stronger the bridge needs to be. Small offense: small bridge. Big offense: big bridge.

Many years ago my relationship with my wife, Lisa, melted down. It revolved around my being a workaholic. She wanted more of my emotional presence, not just my checking in at suppertime and going back to work. It took me a while to see what she was talking about, but when I did, I realized I had a big bridge to build. I needed to prove to her, over and over, and in many ways, that I was sincere about being both physically and emotionally present with her.

The important thing to understand in rebuilding trust is you are not building this bridge for yourself. The offender rarely sees himself or herself as untrustworthy. They tend to build small bridges no matter how big their offense. But you can't build a bridge according to *your* standards if you want to restore a relationship. You need to build a bridge according to the standards of the person you offend. You might think a rope bridge is good enough, but the offended party might say, "Oh no...if we have any future then I need a suspension bridge. You need to prove to me you are trustworthy."

Here are a few additional tips to help build trust with someone you've offended:

- *Apologize well.* This is what I've been talking about so far in this chapter. Doing it *well* builds trust. Doing it half-heartedly actually gives people a reason to get even madder.

- *Stop offending.* This might seem obvious, but some people are in the unhealthy cycle of offend-apologize-forgiveness-offend-apologize-forgiveness, etc. If reconciliation is going to take place, the offense has to stop. Do whatever you need to do to break your habit: get counseling, get prayer, etc. but stop offending. When people see you have built a track record of good behavior, their trust will slowly come back (if they are still around to see your good behavior).

- *Give people permission to not trust you.* If you've proven yourself to be untrustworthy, it's only fair to not expect people to trust you. Tell them that. Let them know it's not their responsibility to trust you, and you will not ask them to trust you until you have earned it. When you give people permission to not trust you, it takes a load of guilt off of them (because they want to trust you but can't), and it shows them you understand (which in turn, builds more trust).

- *Ask what is needed to rebuild trust.* Rebuilding trust does not always require what you might think. You might spend all your time doing one thing when they are looking for another.

So ask, "What can I do to help you trust me again in the future?" In bridge terms, ask the offended what kind of bridge they need you to build: a rope bridge, a covered bridge, or a super structure with lights and video cameras. It's important to agree, in advance, on the bridge that needs to be built.

A word of caution here: the bridge you agree upon should be fair. Some people ask for a super-structure when only a rope bridge is necessary. Their hurt causes them to be unreasonable. Others ask for a super-structure with no intention of ever crossing the bridge. They just want to punish their offender. So, before you launch into a ten-year bridge-building project, make sure you know what you are getting into.

- *Follow through on what you commit to do.* Up until now, it's been all words. If you don't follow through, then your words are empty, and they will make things worse.

- *Make amends.* Fix what's broken, as much as you can. If you are behind on rent, don't just ask to be forgiven; offer your landlord a repayment plan. Take responsibility for whatever loss you have caused people, and pay them back. Making amends goes beyond simple payback to speaking to mutual friends and setting the record straight. Ask their forgiveness as well for any slander or gossip you have spoken about your friend or acquaintance. Until you do this, you will never rebuild trust. On the other hand, if you humble yourself and go out of your way to set the record straight, the person from whom you are seeking forgiveness will see you are sincere and will be quicker to trust you again.

- *Be patient.* Give your friend the time and space they need to trust you again without insisting on it or trying to manipulate them into it. Let your actions speak for you. Continually pointing out how trustworthy you have become will only irritate the person you seek to win over and may backfire.

If you are sincere and persistent, the bridge of trust can be rebuilt. At that time, the responsibility of reconciliation is shared with the offended person. They have to decide if they are willing to walk across the bridge and resume the intimacy your trust offers. You are fully at their mercy.

Sometimes people choose not to cross the bridge out of hurt, anger, or fear. This was a temptation for my wife. A part of her didn't want to trust me again unless I fully understood all the ways I let her down. But she realized that wasn't fair; she felt God asking her to accept my best efforts, even though they might not be all she wanted from me.

It ultimately took several years for me to rebuild her trust. She admits that even then, it was still hard to trust me. In fact, even today she still wonders if she will get my full attention. But she refuses to insist on perfection from me before she trusts. She realizes that risk is inherent to trust; plus, her trust isn't just in me but in God. She trusts that even if I fail to be fully present God will always be there for her.

You Can Do This

The temptation with my four steps to reconciliation is to cut corners.

Like I said, people rarely understand the depth of how much hurt they caused. They are quick to pick up with the relationship before trust has been rebuilt. But if you really want to restore the relationship you generally need to do *more* not *less*.

This all takes great amounts of humility, patience, and self-control. But here's the good news: God wants to give you whatever you need to make things right. The Bible tells us:

> As we know Jesus better, his divine power *gives us* **everything we need** for living a godly life. 2 Peter 1:3 NLT (emphasis added)

> God is able to bless you abundantly, so that in all things at all times, **having all that you need**, you will abound in every good work. 2 Corinthians 9:8 (emphasis added)

In other words, God has given you what you need to restore your relationships (through faith in Jesus and his power in you). You just need to use what you've been given, expecting God to empower you to do the right thing.

If you follow these steps, there is a good chance you will be forgiven. Hopefully, the person you offended will want to do more than forgive: they will want to reconcile with you.. That's the goal. That's the ideal, but whenever you offend someone deeply, you have to hold the relationship loosely. You have no control over the other person, and you must face the reality they may not want to restore the relationship. That's a very real possibility. It's a consequence you must bear without resorting to manipulative tactics like self-pity.

Should this happen, it will hurt, but don't give up. Life can be good again. God is able to help you start over.

Write it down:
- Look at the four parts to reconciling a relationship. *Which parts have you done well? What parts have you done poorly or skipped altogether?*

- *Does this process help explain why your relationships have not been reconciled yet?*

- Write down a plan to work this process with the people you've offended.

Forgiving Yourself

In my work with recovering addicts, I spend half of my time teaching on issues of forgiveness: how to forgive, how to be forgiven, and how to find God's forgiveness. One day, I finished my teaching on God's forgiveness and felt pretty good about it. I presented what I thought was an ironclad case for why God's forgiveness is free and unconditional. When I asked for comments Angie said, "I understand

God's forgiveness. I don't have a problem with that. I just can't forgive myself."

Her response threw me off a bit. I assumed if you accept God's forgiveness you would automatically forgive yourself. But as I thought about it more, it made sense. It's probably true in my own: I know God forgives me, but when I mess up I feel it necessary to beat myself up for a while. God's not ashamed of me, but I am.

Angie lived with the regret of losing her children. Her chronic addiction to drugs and alcohol caused her to lose custody to her ex-boyfriend. She now lives under her own harsh judgment as she continually reflects on the poor choices she made leading up to the loss of her children.

Angie is not alone. Many people just can't seem to shake their self-accusations for past failure. It's as if they choose to stay stuck in life as a means of self-punishment. It's one of the few things they can do to pay for what they've done wrong. But no one is made to live under the weight of guilt. We all need to learn how to forgive ourselves so we can move on in life and achieve better things.

Over the next two chapters I want to answer two questions:
Why should I forgive myself?
How can I forgive myself?

Seven Reasons Why You Should Forgive Yourself

My simple definition for forgiveness is "giving up the right to get even." This applies to us as well as others. We often try to "get even" with ourselves through self-punishment. Here are seven reasons to help you stop doing that:

1. Forgiving Yourself Is Free

A man wrote me the other day and said he finds it hard to forgive himself because he doesn't think he deserves it. I wrote back telling him that he *doesn't* deserve it. No one does. That's why it's called "grace" (which means gift). If we deserved gifts they wouldn't be gifts, they'd be payment. So just enjoy God's gift of forgiveness, and thank him for his kindness to you.

2. Forgiving Yourself Reclaims Your Story

When you refuse to forgive yourself it's like you embrace the past. You choose to accept a bad snapshot of your life as your eternal identity. By forgiving yourself you burn that snapshot and create a whole new photo album. You tell a new story…a better story.

3. Forgiving Yourself Brings You Close To God

Grace is God's gift that has the power to change any situation for good. You can keep yourself at a distance from grace and stay the same for the rest of your life. Or you can accept God's grace, and let it change you. When you do, you encounter the living God. Imagine seeing God effect change in your life day after day. It's pretty exciting.

4. Forgiving Yourself Can Be A Defining Moment

Not forgiving yourself is a form of self-punishment. If God won't punish you then you have to do it. But what if you took that same energy and put it into something positive? Instead of beating yourself up, what if you use your failure as a turning point? What if you use your failure as the motivating factor you've needed to put your life back on track?

In Jerry Sittser's book, *A Grace Disguised*, he makes a powerful statement:
> The experience of loss doesn't have to be the defining moment in our lives. Instead, the defining moment can be our response to the loss. It is not what happens to us that matters so much as what happens in us. [63]

What this means is that your failure can actually lead to a life changing moment. Imagine your funeral. People reflect on your life and say:
> *Everything turned around after their big failure. That was their*

---

[63] Jerry Sittser, *A Grace Disguised*, (Zondervan), p. 45

defining moment. It was like they became a new person.

Isn't that what you want them to say? Do you want them to lament your life saying, *Their failure defined them. They never recovered. It's so sad?*

Is that the legacy you want to leave? It's your choice. It's up to you. By forgiving yourself you can turn the page and write a better story.

5. Forgiving Yourself Adds Value To Your Life

One of the effects of not forgiving yourself is you become less of a person. What I mean is your guilt weighs on you and eats away at you. It's as if you pay for your mistakes on the installment plan, one regret at a time.

Wasn't what you did bad enough? Why do you want to perpetuate that dark history by keeping it alive, punishing yourself time and again?

It's like going to a restaurant. Imagine that I go in and see you eating a meal. Out of kindness I tell the waitress to add your meal to my bill. But even though I pay for it, you insist on paying for it again. That's what happens when you reject God's forgiveness. Jesus paid for your sin once, but you feel the need to keep paying for it, over and over again. How foolish is that?

When you forgive yourself you reverse all of that. You allow yourself to receive good things, and your life takes on new meaning and value. You now have something to offer this world; you can make a contribution. Instead of regret you have pride in your accomplishments. But the longer you wait the less contribution you can make.

6. Forgiving Yourself Benefits Your Loved Ones

By not forgiving yourself, you not only add to the pain of your life, you add to the pain of those you love because you aren't allowing yourself to be fully alive to them. In essence, you cheat them out of the person that you are supposed to be for them. When you punish yourself you punish them too. But forgiving yourself allows you to become the person God called you to be. When that happens you will be a blessing to your loved ones and not just a concern.

7. Forgiving Yourself Allows Transformation To Begin

You may never be able to right your wrong, but you can live well and stop the negative effects of guilt in your life. Forgiving yourself means leaving the past in the past and showing the world the power of God's transforming love and forgiveness.

I've always liked the emphatic words from the book of Hebrews:
> By one sacrifice he has made perfect forever those who are being made holy. Hebrews 10:14

Jesus' death made you perfect... *forever*. Can you receive that?

Two people in the Bible show a stark contrast in terms of receiving God's forgiveness: Peter and Judas. They both failed Jesus by denying him. Judas couldn't forgive himself and committed suicide, while Peter went on to lead the church. No one thinks of Peter as a failure. We think of him as a great church leader. By forgiving himself, Peter was able to live a totally new life.

The same can be said of you. Leave your past by forgiving yourself. Then move on to become the person God made you to be.

Write it down:

- Look through these seven reasons to forgive yourself. *Which ones resonate with you the most?*

- Ask God to expose your false thinking and make these reasons true in your heart.

How to Forgive Yourself

Now that I've explained why you should forgive yourself, here are five ways to do it:

1. Break The Vow

I spoke briefly about vows earlier in the book. Most people who can't forgive themselves made a vow. They decided their actions were so immoral or reprehensible they would never forgive themselves. This is their way of punishing themselves in a manner equal to their offense.

I've learned from my counseling experience that vows are very powerful acts of the will. They are stronger than a belief or a decision. They act almost like a one-way passage in the mind. In other words, once you make a vow, there's almost no going back. People who make vows cease to decide in certain situations. The vow predisposes them to act without the benefit of reason.

For example, if a good friend hurt me in the past, I may vow to never have a close friend again. The decision might protect me in some ways from being hurt, but it also cuts me off from any level of intimacy with people. Imagine God placing someone in my life to help me, encourage me, comfort me, and love me, but my reaction is an immediate wall, pushing him or her away. I won't have anything to do with them because I chose years ago, in the vow, to never have a close friend again. It's almost like a switch was flipped in my brain preventing me from even allowing a friendship to happen. I'm not open to it.

The same thing happens when people vow to never be forgiven. They may not even realize what they have done or don't understand the power the vow has in their life. It literally blocks their ability to show self-kindness.

Because of this, it's important to break the vow. I can't say what takes place when this happens: if it's emotional, psychological, spiritual, or a little of all three, but something happens. I've seen it. When people choose to break a vow, it's like their mind is suddenly given back the ability to choose. Using my previous example, if I break a vow of self-protection, there is a split second of choice. I have the ability to consider, in that moment, the possibility of allowing myself to experience the closeness of a friendship again.

In the same way, if you break the vow to not be forgiven, you will finally be open to at least consider stopping your self-punishment and allowing good things to happen.

How do you break a vow? It's an act of the will before God. Pray something like this:

> Father, I realize I've made a vow to not forgive myself. Looking back, I made it to punish myself for what I've done. But now I see that I was wrong. If you have forgiven me then I should too.

> So Father, I take back my vow to never be forgiven. I break the vow and choose to reopen my mind and heart to everything You have for me. Forgive me for the years I've wasted by being closed off to Your forgiveness. Soften my heart to the truth of Your forgiveness. Let it seep into the deepest part of my being, and heal me of my brokenness. In those split seconds when I have the chance to choose or reject Your forgiveness, please empower me to receive it, and allow good things to happen once again. Thank you Father. Amen.

2. Understand We Are All Failures

Some people insist on beating themselves up. They recognize everyone fails in life, but they believe, against all reason, they are the worst of the worst and deserve harsher treatment. But the Bible tells us:

> There is no difference, for all have sinned and fall short of the glory of God, and are justified freely by his grace through the redemption that came by Christ Jesus. Romans 3:23,24

There is no difference. We are all in the same boat. We have all failed God and fallen short of his standard of perfection. I heard it described once by comparing an Olympic gold medalist swimmer to a novice swimmer. In a pool, the Olympian stands out against the novice. Put them both on the shore of California, tell them to swim to Hawaii, and they will both fall short. The size of the ocean is the great equalizer. The same is true of us all when compared to God.

In a courtroom, some of our lives may be more illegal than others. In a church, some of our lives may be more immoral than others. When compared to God, none of us measure up to his perfection. No one can boast, and no one can take undue guilt upon himself or herself because "there is no difference."

The second part of the verse I quoted above is equally important. It says, "...we are all justified freely by his grace through the redemption that came by Christ Jesus." Yes, we all fail, but more importantly, God forgives us and justifies us. That means we stand before God as if we never failed him. He doesn this for free. It's a gift. And it's made possible, not because of what we have done, but because of what Jesus did. Who are we to object to what God has decided?

In another place in the Bible this point is driven home.
> For it is by grace you have been saved, through faith—and this not from yourselves, it is the gift of God— not by works, so that no one can boast...Ephesians 2:8,9

No one can boast they deserve God's forgiveness, but this also means that no one can claim they can't be forgiven. It may not make sense or feel right, but it's the truth. We need to comply with what is true.

3. Ask Yourself: What Am I Getting?

One day I was teaching a small group about God's forgiveness, and a young girl said she couldn't forgive herself. Out of the blue a question came to me so I asked her, "What are you getting by not forgiving yourself? In other words, what benefit do you receive by not forgiving yourself?" She looked shocked, like she was "busted" or exposed by my question. She paused a minute and said, "If I forgave myself I'd feel the need to change my lifestyle. By not forgiving myself, I have permission to feel sorry for myself and justify using drugs."

Bingo. The clarity she got in that moment was amazing. My question caused her to see the truth behind her inability to forgive herself. The truth was: she wasn't *unable* to forgive herself. She was *unwilling* to change her lifestyle. The forgiveness issue was simply a good "cover" or excuse. My question helped her see the true issue and forced her to deal with the question: *Do I really want to change?*

Since then, I often ask that question of people who can't forgive themselves. Whether people realize it or not, they are getting something by not forgiving themselves. If they are willing to reflect and be honest, they might find the real reason they can't forgive themselves.

4. Consider The Lie

Finally, if you are unable to forgive yourself, you have probably believed some lie at a very deep level. Some possible lies are: *I'm not worthy of being forgiven; God can't love me; or I need to punish myself.* These kinds of lies can't be removed simply by telling yourself the truth. A spiritual surgery needs to take place that only God can do. At my church, we offer a ministry called theophostic prayer that has dramatically impacted people by setting them free from this kind of lie-based thinking. To learn more about theophostic prayer, visit the website www.theophostic.com

Write it down:

- Think back. *Have you ever vowed to not forgive yourself?*

- *Does it help to see there is no difference between people…we are all failures?*

- *Is there any benefit you are getting by not forgiving yourself?*

- *What are some lies you tell yourself that might prevent you from forgiving yourself?*

Chapter Twenty-Two:

Closing Thoughts...

Forgiveness is an ideal. It may seem impossible and therefore not worth the effort. But just because you doubt you can hit the bull's-eye on a target doesn't mean you shoot for the edges. You keep shooting for the center believing that practice makes perfect. Even if you never hit the bulls-eye, you will come much closer to the center than having not tried.

Life is a tension between the ideal and the real. You must decide how to manage that tension. Will you let life events dictate to you, or will you take control of the hand you are dealt? Every day you determine the story your life will tell by the choices you make. I hope you will choose forgiveness as part of your story.

I understand that forgiveness is not a simple formula. It's complex. It's messy. Things don't always go according to plan because we are all too human. But don't let your humanity be an excuse to not try. God wants to make his strength perfect in your weakness. It's the presence of God that bridges the gap between the ideal and the real. Keep trying. Keep praying, and keep expecting God to show up on your behalf in amazing ways.

The Rock

When people come to my seminar they are given a manual and a rock. The manual they understand, but the rock raises some eyebrows. I hand out the rock as an object lesson. You can do three things with rocks:

1. *You can throw rocks* like Jenny did in the opening story, seeking vengeance or some level of retribution. The rock thrower strikes out hoping to find relief by hurting others.

2. *You can put rocks in a backpack*, that is, stuff your feelings and carry your pain through life. That way no one knows about your anger. It makes you look more socially acceptable, but it is also an emotional weight that drains you ever day.

3. *You can take your rocks and build an altar for worship.* In the Old Testament, when God revealed himself to people they would often gather stones and build an altar to remember their encounter with God. This is my hope for you: that you will come to terms with your anger and loss through an encounter with God.

A year after one of my seminars, a woman came to see me about an unrelated matter. Before she spoke about the topic of our meeting, she pulled out a rock and plopped it on my desk. I had no idea what it was, having forgotten she even attended the seminar. She quickly reminded me, saying she put the rock in her purse as a continual reminder of her anger and her need to forgive. It took her a year, but she was finally ready to forgive and move on with her life. She gave me the rock as her way of bringing closure to her anger and finding forgiveness.

I hope the same happens for you, whether it's today, a year from now, or more. I hope a day comes when you can say you are no longer stuck, and you are ready to move on with your life.

I want to close by praying for you.

> *Father, thank You for the person holding this book. They want to move on with their life. Right now they aren't so sure they can do it. They have all kinds of reasons why they can't. I ask on their behalf that You help them to soften their heart, hear from You, and make the heroic choices necessary to get unstuck. Amen.*

Please write and tell me your story about being stuck and hopefully getting unstuck. I love hearing back from people, and I will do my best to answer you.

F. Remy Diederich

remydiederich@yahoo.com

Blog: readingremy.com

Twitter: @FRemy

Facebook: F. Remy Diederich

Chapter Twenty-Three:

Questions and Answers About Getting Unstuck

Forgiveness is not a formula. It's messy. There are many qualifiers that go along with everything I teach in this book. Following are answers to a few common questions that I have gotten regarding forgiveness.

Q: What about the people you love who don't want you to forgive?

A: It's always harder for your friends and family to forgive your offender. They don't understand the dynamics. They feel the need to protect you, fearing what happened will happen again. Try to see the good in what they are doing. Give them permission to let go and not protect you. Also, let them know forgiveness isn't excusing or trust. That's what they fear; you will allow yourself to get hurt again. Assure them that's not true. You are simply choosing to not get back at your offender and let the past control your future. Once they understand this, they will be more at ease. Maybe you can write them a note thanking them for their concern and outlining your perspective.

Q: When does "love" not equal being used, manipulated, and mistreated, and when is it being giving, humble, peace loving,

etc. Sometimes the lines are very blurred!

A: A good understanding of boundaries will help you with this. Everyone needs to know who they are and who they are not: where they stop and the other person starts. Love doesn't mean allowing others to deplete you. If you are being depleted, a day will come when you no longer exist. You will be used up. That can't happen. You need to monitor what fills your tank and what depletes it. You also need to monitor who is stealing from your tank or taking you for granted.

Many people allow themselves to be used by others because of low self-worth; they need the affirmation of others, even if others take advantage of them. Or they sense an obligation to be considered a good person or "good Christian." Be careful with this. If you allow one person to totally drain you, then how can you be available to love others? You might want to ask a close friend to tell you if they see that happening. Get another perspective. Seek counseling for perspective as well.

The answer to your question can be found in the fruit in your life and who is in control of it. If the other person is impacting you more than you are impacting them, then I think you need to make an adjustment.

Q: I have struggled with the "what happens now" after forgiveness has been given. I would love to hear your perspective on how to let go of an unhealthy relationship (sibling, etc.) in a way that still honors God.

A: With family members, the ties and history give you more reason to work at reunion than other relationships; but don't let that coerce you either. Don't feel obligated to get back together or spend every holiday together, etc. Give yourself permission to set boundaries that create distance between you and your family. Just because they are family doesn't give them immediate access to your space. They must earn that right like anyone else.

Be careful not to let family members pressure you to live up to their expectations. I'm amazed at how often people allow their parents to dictate their lives well into adulthood. You can set boundaries respectfully. Your family might resent the boundaries, especially if they aren't used to them, but don't let them intimidate you.

We honor God by respecting the personal space he wants us to have (versus being overwhelmed by unhealthy people) and communicating boundaries in a firm and respectful manner. Don't use boundaries to punish. Don't be cruel. Be firm and consistent.

Q: What if my child is on a self-destructive path? I want to help him, but not enable him. I can't stand the thought of him dying because no one intervened.

A: You can follow the teaching of Jesus who tells us to do three things: go to the person, bring others, and tell it to the church. In other words, keep increasing the intensity of the confrontation in hopes of them changing their lives. Speak directly to them, but don't nag. That only shuts them down. You can perform an intervention with family and friends. This is what causes many people to "see the light." You can even call the police if you think they are in danger of harming themselves. By all means, don't stand by quietly. But ultimately it is up to them. You can't solve their problems for them. They have to take responsibility for themselves. And if they die, you can't carry that weight. You shouldn't carry it now either. I realize that's easier said than done.

Q: Is everything forgivable? Affairs?

A: Everything is forgivable, even affairs. Some people don't want to be forgiven. Or some people want to work it both ways. They want the marriage, but they don't want to change their behavior or ask to be forgiven. Refer to what I said about forgiveness not meaning trust. Forgiveness is free. Trust is earned. You can forgive an affair but not trust someone until they rebuild your trust. Forgiveness doesn't necessarily mean you should stay together. Reunion requires two people working hard over time.

Q: What do you do when someone won't forgive you?

A: First, go through my process on how to be reconciled. They might not forgive you because you are continually offending them. Do your best, but you can't force people to forgive you. Pray for them and give them space. You should be aware that the relationship might be lost. Even if that happens it's not the end of the world. God is not limited. Good things can still happen to you.

More Questions?
Getting unstuck is complicated. This book is meant to help but there are so many exceptions to every rule. I welcome your questions at remydiederich@yahoo.com. Also, check out readingremy.com where I have many blog posts about forgiveness.

Recommended Reading List

- *A Lasting Promise*, Stanley, Trathen, McCain, Bryan, Jossey-Bass
- *The Anger Workbook*, Les Carter, Frank Minirth, Nelson Publishing
- *The Art of Forgiving*, Lewis Smedes, Moorings Press
- *Boundaries*, Henry Cloud, John Townsend, Zondervan
- *Choosing to Live the Blessing*, John Trent, WaterBrook Press
- *Christian Counseling*, Gary Collins, Word
- *Emotions Revealed*, Paul Ekman, Owl Books
- *Faces of Forgiveness, The: Searching for Wholeness and Salvation*, F. LeRon Shults, Ph.D. and Steven J. Sandage, Ph.D., Baker Academic
- *Free of Charge*, Miroslav Volf, Zondervan
- *Forgiveness is a Choice*, Robert Enright, APA Lifetools
- *Forgive and Forget*, Lewis Smedes, Harpercollins Publishing
- *Forgive to Live*, Dr. Dick Tibitts, Thomas Nelson
- *To Forgive is Human*, Michael McCullough, Steven Sandage, Everett Worthington, IVP
- *Forgiving the Unforgivable*, Beverly Flanigan, MacMillan Press
- *Happiness is a Choice*, Frank Minirth and Paul Meier, Baker Books
- *How to Really Love Your Teenager*, Ross Campbell, Victor Press
- *Making Love Last Forever*, Gary Smalley, Word
- *Necessary Changes*, Henry Cloud, HarperCollins
- *Rebuilding Your Private World*, Gordon MacDonald, Oliver-Nelson Press
- *The Faces of Forgiveness*, F. LeRon Shults and Steven J. Sandage, Baker Academic
- *The Safest Place on Earth*, Larry Crabb, Word

Acknowledgements

I've had a desire to write for years, but the question always came to mind: *What can I possibly say that hasn't already been said?* That's a pretty convincing argument. The answer: Nothing! Plus, writing and publishing a book takes an incredible amount of time. As a busy pastor, I don't have any free hours at the end of my day.

A few years ago, I wrote two curriculum's to teach at Arbor Place Treatment Center. I made a halfhearted attempt at getting them published, but the whole process was too overwhelming, so I gave it up. I told God, "If you ever want me to publish a book you'll have to send someone to me that is willing to champion the process. Otherwise, I give up. I don't have the time."

Five years went by and surprisingly someone did come along to champion the publishing of my books. Jason Brooks was in the early stages of launching Media Buzz Hub and was looking for authors. Being a friend, I told him about my two works and offered him the chance to practice on me. I had no intention of ever getting published, so there was no loss if nothing came of it. That launched both Media Buzz Hub as well as my book career.

Our first book was **Healing the Hurts of Your Past**...*a guide to overcoming the pain of shame*, and the second book is the one you hold in your hand.

I want to thank God for bringing me Jason, and I want to thank Jason for his drive and energy to not only get my books into the world but to also help other authors do the same. Jason, you are a lot of fun and a huge encouragement to me. Thanks for all of your practical help as well as Becky's.

Much of my material was developed at Arbor Place Treatment Center through countless small group discussions. I love the clients that we serve. I love helping them get unstuck by offering them simple wisdom and the grace of a loving God. Many of them end up at Cedarbrook and have become my friends.

Speaking of Cedarbrook, where would I be without this church? Twenty dreamers and I started Cedarbrook Church in 2003, and it is now a thriving congregation. Much of what I write flows from the relationships that I'm a part of there. I have the best leadership team (Mike Glapa, Mark and Beverly Deyo-Svendsen, Sarah Anderson, Tracey Sorenson, Swen Erickson, Don Prochnow, Chris Ehlert, Jim Walker, Jeremy Burns, Mark Lewis) and staff (Carla Reed, Kyle Gunderson, Brenda Brewer, Cassandra Smith, Christine Thomsen, Pam Brekke, Dave Johnson, Stephanie Demers, and Jayne Rechtzigel).

I want to offer a special thanks to my friends Jim and Patti Walker who believed in me way back when I was milking cows and teaching Sunday school. Your partnership in all of this is a true blessing. Also thanks to Byron Anderson for his keen insight and servant's heart. And hats off to those who read an early version of this book and gave me constructive feedback (Bob and Lori Pope, Elli Hunt, Bill and Kris Tice, Alison Glapa, Sandy Buckner, and Bobbi Graffunde). Alison and Sandy get three stars for the fine grammar edits and four stars go to Bobbi for not only the grammatical edits but the encouragement and caution throughout the text. I'm given to overstatement and Bobbi caught me every time.

To Jay and Pam, I'm now available again for golf and football parties. And no, my next book is not, *How to Lose Friends by Writing Books All the Time.*

Of course, no one has ever supported me as much as my wife, Lisa. We have gone through many seasons of highs and lows together. She has been my greatest encourager and joy. Thanks for working with me throughout our marriage to never accept "stuck" as the norm, but to pursue an intimacy that only God can provide. Thanks for patiently allowing me to take time away from vacations, evenings at home, and my "to-do" list to write, and rewrite, this book!

About the Author

F. Remy Diederich is the founding pastor of Cedarbrook Church in Menomonie, Wisconsin. He also consults at the Arbor Place Treatment Center in areas of anger/forgiveness and shame/self-worth. He is available to speak to your group on request.

You might also be interested in Remy's first book ***Healing the Hurts of Your Past…a guide to overcoming the pain of shame.***

Please visit his website at readingremy.com for more life changing resources from Remy.

You may contact Remy at <u>remydiederich@yahoo.com</u> .

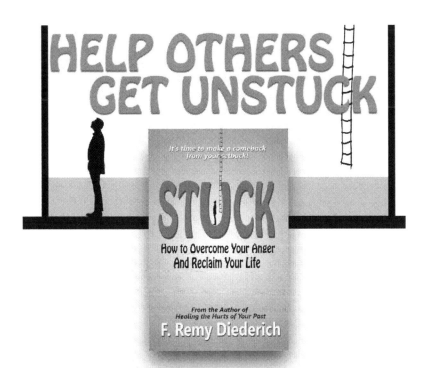

"In STUCK, Remy Diederich offers the same healing voice of grace and truth as he did in HEALING THE HURTS OF YOUR PAST.
Having previously helped us overcome the pain of our shame, in a gentle and loving way, Remy now comes alongside as a friend and gives us what we need to become unstuck.

-Mark Halvorsen
News Director/Host of Front Page 103.7 WWIB

Share this book at your church or in your recovery ministry.
Take advantage of special bulk pricing by visiting
www.readingremy.com/stuck

MAKE YOUR COMBACK TODAY!

God used your writings to significantly restore my soul, my faith in the church, and my internal perspective on God. Even my wife and our two sons regularly said, "What in the world are you reading? You are a different man than you were before." Thank you for allowing God's inspiration to flow through you.

-KEN DEPEAL

Share this book at your church or in your pastoral care ministry. Take advantage of special bulk pricing by visiting www.readingremy.com/exile

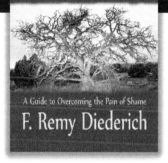

"Remy Diederich has done a masterful job of weaving theological and psychological concepts together in a way that makes sense."

Take others through the book that helps connect the dots of the hurts and pains of the past to unleash a new life of freedom in Christ

Share this book at your church or in your recovery ministry
Take advantage of special bulk pricing by visiting
www.readingremy.com/healing

Made in the USA
Columbia, SC
22 March 2020